Editor
Erica N. Russikoff, M.A.

Contributing Editor
Michael H. Levin, M.A., N.B.C.T.

Illustrators
Mark Mason
Renée Christine Yates

Cover Artist
Tony Carrillo

Editor in Chief
Ina Massler Levin, M.A.

Creative Director
Karen J. Goldfluss, M.S. Ed.

Imaging
Rosa C. See

Publisher

Mary D. Smith, M.S. Ed.

W9-CHW-189

TCR 8845

Grade 5

Summertime Learning

Prepare Your Child for Fifth Grade

With 8 weeks worth of reading, writing, math and just plain fun!

Includes over **300** stickers!

Teacher Created Resources

Teacher Created Resources, Inc.

12621 Western Avenue
Garden Grove, CA 92841
www.teachercreated.com

ISBN: 978-1-4206-8845-0

©2010 Teacher Created Resources, Inc.

Reprinted, 2020 (PO602782)

Made in U.S.A.

Teacher Created Resources

Table of Contents

A Message From the National Summer Learning Association 4
How to Use This Book 5–6
Standards and Skills 7–9
Reward Chart 10

Week 1 Activities 11–20

Monday	Math: *All About Money*
	Reading: *At the Top*
Tuesday	Math: *Spending Money*
	Writing: *Road Trips*
Wednesday	Math: *Clever Inventions*
	Reading: *Fun in the Sun*
Thursday	Math: *Doughnuts*
	Writing: *My Memories*
Friday	Friday Fun: *Weather Wise, Running with Riddles*

Week 2 Activities 21–30

Monday	Math: *What a Hit!*
	Writing: *What Happened?*
Tuesday	Math: *Go Around*
	Reading: *Medical School*
Wednesday	Math: *A Division Crossword*
	Writing: *Story Boxes*
Thursday	Math: *Food Challenge*
	Reading: *Green Thumb*
Friday	Friday Fun: *Favorite Meals, Decode the Plates*

Week 3 Activities 31–40

Monday	Math: *Solve Them*
	Reading: *Madame Curie*
Tuesday	Math: *Patterns*
	Writing: *Diamante Poems*
Wednesday	Math: *Vehicles Sold*
	Reading: *The Best Definition*
Thursday	Math: *Family Vacations*
	Writing: *Pros and Cons*
Friday	Friday Fun: *What's the Message?, Silly Sayings*

Week 4 Activities 41–50

Monday	Math: *Number Crossword*
	Writing: *Cause and Effect*
Tuesday	Math: *Multiplication Mystery*
	Reading: *Coral Reef*
Wednesday	Math: *Read-a-Thon*
	Writing: *More Cause and Effect*
Thursday	Math: *Games and Birds*
	Reading: *What Happened Next?*
Friday	Friday Fun: *ABC Puzzlers, Hidden Animals*

Week 5 Activities 51–60

Monday	Math: *Favorite Sports*
	Reading: *Electricity*
Tuesday	Math: *City Grid*
	Writing: *Join Them*
Wednesday	Math: *Just the Area*
	Reading: *Same Sound*

Table of Contents

(cont.)

Week 5 Activities *(cont.)*

Thursday	Math: *Real World Geometry*	
	Writing: *Fact or Opinion?*	
Friday	Friday Fun: *Droodles, If True, Then Do*	

Week 6 Activities 61–70

Monday	Math: *Meet the Merkles*
	Writing: *Let's Begin*
Tuesday	Math: *Rent an Apartment*
	Reading: *Micro- and Mini-*
Wednesday	Math: *How Many Degrees?*
	Writing: *Fill the Gaps*
Thursday	Math: *Add the Lengths*
	Reading: *Separate Them*
Friday	Friday Fun: *Map Madness!, Race to the Finish*

Week 7 Activities 71–80

Monday	Math: *Numbers and Dollars*
	Reading: *Story Types*
Tuesday	Math: *Math Grab Bag*
	Writing: *So Personal*
Wednesday	Math: *Many Variables*
	Reading: *Air Tour*
Thursday	Math: *Shade and Show*
	Writing: *Which Kind?*
Friday	Friday Fun: *Idiom Crossword, Take the Plunge*

Week 8 Activities 81–90

Monday	Math: *Draggum and Pushum*
	Writing: *What Are They Doing?*
Tuesday	Math: *The Eatery*
	Reading: *Past Poetry*
Wednesday	Math: *Great Volume*
	Writing: *TV Review*
Thursday	Math: *Going the Distance*
	Reading: *Find the Clues*
Friday	Friday Fun: *The World's Best, More Droodles*

All About Me 91

Summer Reading List 92–94

Fun Ways to Love Books 95

Bookmark Your Words 96

Read-Together Chart 97

Journal Topics 98

Learning Experiences 99

Web Sites 100–101

Handwriting Chart 102

Proofreading Marks 103

Multiplication Chart 104

Measurement Tools 105

Answer Key 106–112

A Message From the
National Summer Learning Association

Dear Parents,

Did you know that all young people experience learning losses when they don't engage in educational activities during the summer? That means some of what they've spent time learning over the preceding school year evaporates during the summer months. However, summer learning loss *is* something that you can help prevent. Summer is the perfect time for fun and engaging activities that can help children maintain and grow their academic skills. Here are just a few:

- Read with your child every day. Visit your local library together, and select books on subjects that interest your child.

- Ask your child's teacher for recommendations of books for summer reading. The Summer Reading List in this publication is a good start.

- Explore parks, nature preserves, museums, and cultural centers.

- Consider every day as a day full of teachable moments. Measuring in recipes and reviewing maps before a car trip are ways to learn or reinforce a skill. Use the Learning Experiences in the back of this book for more ideas.

- Each day, set goals to accomplish. For example, do five math problems or read a chapter in a book.

- Encourage your child to complete the activities in books, such as *Summertime Learning*, to help bridge the summer learning gap.

Our vision is for every child to be safe, healthy, and engaged in learning during the summer. Learn more at *www.summerlearning.org* and *www.summerlearningcampaign.org*.

Have a *memorable* summer!

Ron Fairchild
Chief Executive Officer
National Summer Learning Association

How to Use This Book

As a parent, you know that summertime is a time for fun and learning. So it is quite useful that fun and learning can go hand in hand when your child uses *Summertime Learning*.

There are many ways to use this book effectively with your child. We list three ideas on page 6. (See "Day by Day," "Pick and Choose," and "All of a Kind.") You may choose one way on one day, and, on another day, choose something else.

Book Organization

Summertime Learning is organized around an eight-week summer vacation period. For each weekday, there are two lessons. Each Monday through Thursday, there is a math lesson. Additionally, during the odd-numbered weeks, there is a reading lesson on Monday and Wednesday and a writing lesson on Tuesday and Thursday. During the even-numbered weeks, these lessons switch days. (Reading lessons are on Tuesday and Thursday, and writing lessons are on Monday and Wednesday.) Friday features two Friday Fun activities (one typically being a puzzle). The calendar looks like this:

Day	Week 1	Week 2	Week 3	Week 4	Week 5	Week 6	Week 7	Week 8
M	Math Reading	Math Writing	Math Reading	Math Writing	Math Reading	Math Writing	Math Reading	Math Writing
T	Math Writing	Math Reading	Math Writing	Math Reading	Math Writing	Math Reading	Math Writing	Math Reading
W	Math Reading	Math Writing	Math Reading	Math Writing	Math Reading	Math Writing	Math Reading	Math Writing
Th	Math Writing	Math Reading	Math Writing	Math Reading	Math Writing	Math Reading	Math Writing	Math Reading
F	Friday Fun Friday Fun	Friday Fun Friday Fun	Friday Fun Friday Fun	Friday Fun Friday Fun	Friday Fun Friday Fun	Friday Fun Friday Fun	Friday Fun Friday Fun	Friday Fun Friday Fun

How to Use This Book
(cont.)

Day by Day

You can have your child do the activities in order, beginning on the first Monday of summer vacation. He or she can complete the two lessons provided for each day. It does not matter if math, reading, or writing is completed first. The pages are designed so that each day of the week's lessons are back to back. The book is also perforated. This gives you the option of tearing the pages out for your child to work on. If you opt to have your child tear out the pages, you might want to store the completed pages in a special folder or three-ring binder that your child decorates.

Pick and Choose

You may find that you do not want to have your child work strictly in order. Feel free to pick and choose any combination of pages based on your child's needs and interests.

All of a Kind

Perhaps your child needs more help in one area than another. You may opt to have him or her work only on math, reading, or writing.

Keeping Track

A Reward Chart is included on page 10 of this book, so you and your child can keep track of the activities that have been completed. This page is designed to be used with the stickers provided. Once your child has finished a page, have him or her put a sticker on the castle. If you don't want to use stickers for this, have your child color in a circle each time an activity is completed.

The stickers can also be used on the individual pages. As your child finishes a page, let him or her place a sticker in the sun at the top of the page. If he or she asks where to begin the next day, simply have him or her start on the page after the last sticker.

There are enough stickers to use for both the Reward Chart and the sun on each page. Plus, there are extra stickers for your child to enjoy.

Standards and Skills

Each activity in *Summertime Learning* meets one or more of the following standards and skills*. Visit *http://www.teachercreated.com/standards/* for correlations to the Common Core State Standards. The activities in this book are designed to help your child reinforce the skills learned during fourth grade, as well as introduce new skills that will be learned in fifth grade.

Language Arts Standards

- ✿ Uses the general skills and strategies of the writing process
- ✿ Uses the stylistic and rhetorical aspects of writing
- ✿ Uses grammatical and mechanical conventions in written composition
- ✿ Gathers and uses information for research purposes
- ✿ Uses the general skills and strategies of the reading process
- ✿ Uses the reading skills and strategies to understand and interpret a variety of literary texts
- ✿ Uses the reading skills and strategies to understand a variety of informational texts
- ✿ Uses listening and speaking strategies for different purposes
- ✿ Uses viewing skills and strategies to understand and interpret visual media
- ✿ Understands the characteristics and components of the media

Mathematics Standards

- ✿ Uses a variety of strategies in the problem-solving process
- ✿ Understands and applies basic and advanced properties of the concepts of numbers
- ✿ Uses basic and advanced procedures while performing the processes of computation
- ✿ Understands and applies basic and advanced properties of the concepts of measurement
- ✿ Understands and applies basic and advanced properties of the concepts of geometry
- ✿ Understands and applies basic and advanced concepts of statistics and data analysis
- ✿ Understands and applies basic and advanced concepts of probability
- ✿ Understands and applies basic and advanced properties of functions and algebra

Writing Skills

- ✿ Uses strategies to draft and revise written work
- ✿ Evaluates own and other's writing
- ✿ Use strategies to edit and publish written work
- ✿ Uses strategies to write for a variety of purposes
- ✿ Writes expository compositions
- ✿ Writes expressive compositions
- ✿ Writes in response to literature

Standards and Skills
(cont.)

Writing Skills *(cont.)*

- ✿ Uses descriptive language that clarifies and enhances ideas
- ✿ Uses paragraph form in writing
- ✿ Use a variety of sentence structures in writing
- ✿ Uses pronouns in written compositions
- ✿ Uses nouns in written compositions
- ✿ Uses verbs in written compositions
- ✿ Uses conventions of capitalization in written compositions
- ✿ Uses conventions of punctuation in written compositions
- ✿ Uses conventions of spelling in written compositions

Reading Skills

- ✿ Establishes a purpose for reading
- ✿ Makes, confirms, and revises simple predictions about what will be found in a text
- ✿ Uses a variety of context clues to decode unknown words
- ✿ Understands level-appropriate reading vocabulary
- ✿ Monitors own reading strategies and makes modifications as needed
- ✿ Understands the author's purpose or point of view
- ✿ Uses reading skills and strategies to understand a variety of literary passages and texts
- ✿ Knows the defining characteristics of a variety of literary forms and genres
- ✿ Understands the basic concept of plot
- ✿ Makes inferences or draws conclusions about a character's qualities and actions
- ✿ Understands the way in which language is used in literary texts
- ✿ Makes connections between characters or simple events in a literary work and people or events in his or her own life
- ✿ Uses text organizers to determine the main ideas
- ✿ Summarizes and paraphrases information in texts
- ✿ Uses prior knowledge and experience to understand and respond to new information
- ✿ Understands structural patterns or organization in informational texts
- ✿ Responds to questions and comments
- ✿ Understands different messages conveyed through visual media
- ✿ Understands the different ways in which people are stereotyped in visual media
- ✿ Knows the main formats and characteristics of familiar media

Standards and Skills
(cont.)

Mathematics Skills

- ✿ Represents problem situations in a variety of forms
- ✿ Understands that some ways of representing a problem are more helpful than others
- ✿ Understands equivalent forms of basic percents, fractions, and decimals
- ✿ Understands the basic meaning of place value
- ✿ Understands the relative magnitude and relationships among whole numbers, fractions, decimals, and mixed numbers
- ✿ Multiplies and divides whole numbers
- ✿ Adds, subtracts, multiplies, and divides decimals
- ✿ Adds and subtracts simple fractions
- ✿ Uses specific strategies to estimate computations and to check the reasonableness of computational results
- ✿ Determines the effects of addition, subtraction, multiplication, and division on size and order of numbers
- ✿ Understands the properties of and the relationships among addition, subtraction, multiplication, and division
- ✿ Solves real-world problems involving number operations
- ✿ Knows the language of basic operations
- ✿ Knows the approximate size of basic standard units and relationships between them
- ✿ Understands relationships between measures
- ✿ Understands basic properties of figures
- ✿ Predicts and verifies the effect of combining, subdividing, and changing basic shapes
- ✿ Uses motion geometry to understand geometric relationships
- ✿ Understands that data represent specific pieces of information about real-world objects or activities
- ✿ Organizes and displays data in simple bar graphs, pie charts, and line graphs
- ✿ Understands that data comes in many different forms and that collecting, organizing, and displaying data can be done in many ways
- ✿ Understands that when predictions are based on what is known about the past, one must assume that conditions stay the same from the past event
- ✿ Uses basic sample spaces to describe and predict events
- ✿ Knows that a variable is a letter or symbol that stands for one or more numbers
- ✿ Solves simple, open sentences involving operations on whole numbers
- ✿ Understands that numbers and the operations performed on them can be used to describe things in the real world and predict what might occur

* Standards and Skills used with permission from McREL (Copyright 2009, McREL. Midcontinent Research for Education and Learning. Address: 4601 DTC Boulevard, Suite 500, Denver, CO 80237. Telephone: 303-337-0990. Web site: www.mcrel.org/standards-benchmarks)

Reward Chart

All About Money

Directions: Solve each problem using multiplication or division. Show your work.

1. If one football costs $21.45, how much would nine footballs cost?

$$
\begin{array}{r}
{}^{2}21\overset{4}{4}.\overset{5}{4}\overset{1}{5}0 \\
2\ 6\ 4\ 5 \\
\hline
1\ 93.05
\end{array}
$$

Nine footballs would cost _193.05_.

2. To keep their children active, a group of seven parents rented a giant bouncer for $84.63. They split the cost evenly. How much did each parent pay?

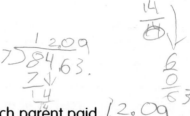

$$
\begin{array}{r}
12.09 \\
7\overline{)84.63.} \\
7\downarrow \\
14 \\
14
\end{array}
$$

Each parent paid _12.09_.

3. A bag of jacks cost $2.79 at the Toys-4-Me store. How much would it cost for thirty bags?

Thirty bags would cost _____.

4. A boys' basketball team with five players bought a hoop and rim for $59.95 and split the cost evenly. How much did each player pay?

Each player paid _____.

5. A bag of marbles cost $2.79. A group of five teachers bought twenty bags of marbles and split the cost evenly. How much did each teacher pay?

Each teacher paid _____.

6. A checkerboard game costs $12.50 at the Grins and Games store. How much would it cost to buy twenty checkerboard games?

Twenty checkerboard games would

cost _____.

At the Top

Directions: Read the story, and then circle the correct answers below.

It is an exhilarating feeling to stand at the top of a mountain and look down. There are amazing views. You can tell by looking at a mountain which plants can grow at different heights. The higher you go up the mountain, the colder it is. For every 820 feet you climb, the temperature drops one degree. If you look at the very top of a high mountain, there is usually no or very little vegetation or plants there. Icy wind blows and prevents trees from growing. When mountains get higher than 8,200 feet, there is a timberline. Trees cannot grow above the timberline.

The trees along the mountainside help to protect the mountain soil. This prevents the mountain soil from eroding. When there is too much erosion, there are problems with flooding and landslides. In the wintertime, these cleared-off areas can trigger avalanches.

It is very common to see conifer trees growing on mountains. Most conifers are called evergreens, which means that they stay green all of the time. They do not lose their leaves like other trees. The leaves on evergreens are needles. When old needles fall off, they are replaced with new ones. Conifers are able to handle the harsh weather conditions of the mountains. They can survive the cold and the elements.

There are also other types of trees that grow on mountains. In lower portions of the mountain, you can find chestnut, oak, and maple trees.

1. What is this passage mainly about?
   a. how tall mountains can get
   b. how trees grow below the timberline
   c. how conifer trees lose their needles and then replace them
   d. the different types of trees that can grow on mountains

2. Why does the temperature get cooler the higher you go up a mountain?
   a. The temperature drops as air pressure rises.
   b. The temperature drops because there are no trees.
   c. The temperature drops because of the higher elevation.
   d. The temperature drops because conifer trees can't grow above the timberline.

3. According to the passage, what are the two main factors that create harsh conditions?
   a. snow and hail
   b. sleet and snow
   c. wind and cold temperatures
   d. cold temperatures and hail

Spending Money

Directions: Ginger receives a $10.00-a-week allowance. The pie chart shows how Ginger spends her money.

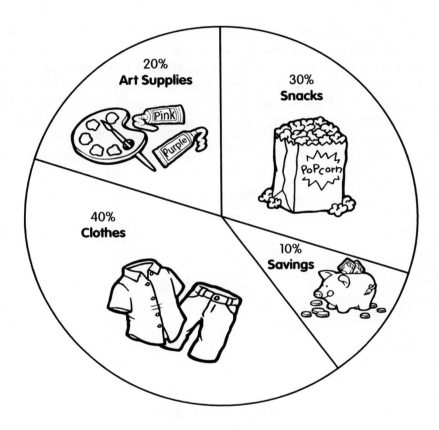

1. How much money does Ginger spend on each category of items?

   Art Supplies: _____   Snacks: _____

   Clothes: _____   Savings: _____

2. If the average month has 4 weeks, how much money does Ginger save in a month? _____

3. If the average year has 52 weeks, how much money does Ginger spend on art

   supplies in a year? _____

4. If Ginger uses her clothing money for a new winter coat that costs $25.00, how many weeks

   will it take for Ginger to have enough money to pay for it?_____

Road Trips

Directions: Read the following paragraph. Then, identify the main idea, and write two supporting details. Write them in the graphic organizer below.

> To have a successful road trip, you must make proper traveling plans. First, you should decide where you want to go and how long you want your trip to be. Next, you must plan your traveling route on a map. You may even want to check your route on several maps to make sure that you have chosen the best plan. Thirdly, you must locate hotels, camping grounds, or relatives' and friends' homes where you will stay. It is always a good idea to call and make reservations ahead of time. Finally, you are ready to pack your belongings, jump in the car, and sit back and enjoy your vacation!

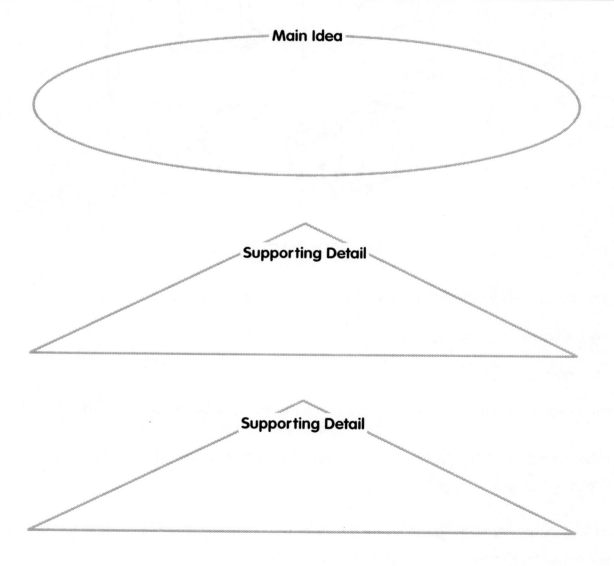

Main Idea

Supporting Detail

Supporting Detail

Clever Inventions

Directions: Read the clues at the bottom of the page to discover the year each item was invented. Then, complete the table.

Inventions for the Last One Hundred Years

Year	Invention
1903	Motorized plane
_____	Ice-cream cone
_____	Oreo® cookies
_____	Television
_____	Pre-sliced bread
1949	Silly Putty®
1955	Frozen TV dinners
_____	Early Internet
1972	Handheld calculator
1973	Cellular phone
_____	Rollerblade® skates
_____	Compact discs (CDs)
_____	Animal cloning—Dolly the sheep

- ✿ Dolly the sheep was cloned 90 years after the Wright Brothers flew the first motorized plane.

- ✿ Rollerblade® skates were invented 13 years before Dolly the sheep was cloned.

- ✿ Pre-sliced bread was introduced 50 years before Rollerblade® skates.

- ✿ Compact discs came 51 years after pre-sliced bread.

- ✿ Oreo® cookies have been around 70 years longer than compact discs.

- ✿ The Internet came along 66 years after the Wright Brothers flew their plane.

- ✿ The first television was made three years before pre-sliced bread was made.

- ✿ The Wright Brothers flew their plane one year before the first ice-cream cone was made.

Fun in the Sun

Directions: Read the following story. Use the Mini Dictionary to help you fill in the missing words.

Mini Dictionary

collapse—fall down

exhausted—very tired, fatigued

kayak—a small canoe

muscles—parts of the body that are used for movement and strength

navigate—ride around, sail

What a day! All of the _____ in my back and arms ache! I'm not moving from
1

my bed for the rest of the week, I tell you!

It started at 8:00 this morning—which is way too early if you ask me. It was my cousin's idea

to take the _____ out on the river behind our cabin. We must have been
2

paddling around out there for hours in the hot sun. I was totally _____
3

by about 9:30, but we stayed out on the lake until almost noon. At one point, we had to

_____ around a big pile of logs that were floating in the river. That did me in.
4

By the time we got home, I was ready to _____ on my bed and go to sleep.
5

Directions: On the blank, write the letter of the dictionary word next to the idea it best matches.

_____ 6. The bigger these are, the stronger a person is.   a. kayak

_____ 7. Use this to move down a stream.   b. collapse

_____ 8. Do this when you are tired.   c. navigate

_____ 9. Do this when you are moving along the water.   d. muscles

_____ 10. You feel this way when you've worked too hard.   e. exhausted

Doughnuts

Directions: Use your mathematics skills to solve the word problems below. Remember, all answers involving money have a dollar sign and decimal point.

Price List

Creamy Dream	$1.99	Plum Nuts Filled	$1.75
Doggy Doughnut	$2.49	Round Mound	$2.99
Juicy Jelly	$2.25	Tiger Twist	$1.49

1. Your best friend bought a Doggy Doughnut and a Plum Nuts Filled for his breakfast. How much did it cost him? _____

2. How much less does it cost for a Plum Nuts Filled than for a Round Mound?

   _____

3. You bought a Tiger Twist. How much change did you get from a $10.00 bill? _____

4. A group of six teenagers spent $24.60. They split the cost evenly. How much money did each teenager pay? _____

5. Your coach bought a Creamy Dream, a Juicy Jelly, and a Round Mound. How much did he spend? _____

6. A grandfather bought each of his nine grandchildren a Plum Nuts Filled. How much did it cost him? _____

7. The fifth-grade teacher bought thirty Juicy Jelly doughnuts for her class. How much did it cost her? _____

8. The girls' soccer coach bought fifteen Round Mounds for her team. How much did she pay?

   _____

9. A group of twenty teenagers bought $98.80 worth of doughnuts and split the cost evenly among them. How much did each teenager pay? _____

10. Mike bought one of each doughnut. How much did Mike spend? _____

My Memories

Directions: Gather information about yourself. Then, write the information in paragraph form.

My name is _____.

I was born in _____.

A funny story about me is _____

_____

_____

When I was a baby, I used to play with _____

_____

_____

This year, I want to learn how to _____

_____

_____

Some of my friends are _____

_____

_____

My favorite foods are _____

_____

_____

My pets or toys are _____

_____

_____

Some of my talents include _____

_____

_____

Something I like about me is _____

_____

_____

Life-Line
Born
Year 1
Year 2
Year 3
Year 4
Year 5
Year 6
Year 7
Year 8

Weather Wise

Directions: Hidden in each sentence is a word that a meteorologist might use in a weather report. Each "weather word" can be found either in the middle of a word or by combining the end of one word with the beginning of the next. Underline the "weather word" in each sentence.

Example: He i<u>s now</u> in fifth grade. (weather word = snow)

1. There was mildew in the bathroom.

2. They had to move the show indoors.

3. The cannon was shot during the Civil War.

4. The tamales were rather spicy.

5. I'd like to sail the seas on an inner tube!

6. She is unlikely to pass the test.

7. They were about to scold Jess for being late.

8. Heather is learning to speak Spanish.

9. I sprained my ankle at the game.

10. The Thunderbird car was made by Ford.

11. In public, loud noises can be distracting.

12. The monster has torn a door off of its hinges.

13. That cat has clearly annoyed the dog.

14. Threats of war might encourage the two countries to negotiate.

Running with Riddles

Directions: Solve the riddles below.

1. Where does August come before July?

2. What is black and white and read all over?

3. What comes next in this pattern: o t t f f s s?

4. How many letters are in the alphabet?

5. What state is surrounded the most by water?

6. What occurs once in a minute, twice in a moment, and never in a thousand years?

7. A mother has nine children. She says that half of them are boys. How can this be true?

8. A man was born in 1947. He is healthy and strong today at 27. How is this possible?

9. Sandra is running a race and passes the person in 2nd place. What place is she in now?

10. I can be thrown off a tall building and won't break. I can be thrown into a car, and still I won't break. But if you throw me in a river or the ocean, I will break into pieces. What am I?

What a Hit!

Week 2: Monday

Directions: The double line graph shows the number of home runs hit by the home run leader in both leagues over a ten-year period. Study the graph, and answer the questions below.

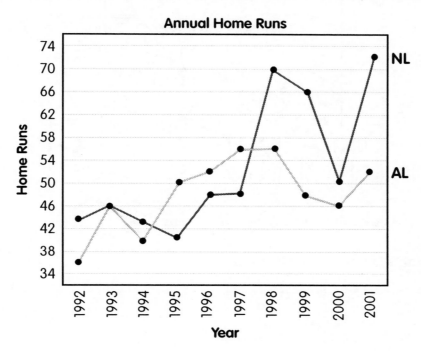

1. In which year were the most home runs hit by one league? <u>2001</u>

2. In which year did the American League (AL) leader and the National League (NL) leader hit the same number of home runs? <u>1993</u>

3. In which two years did the American League leader hit 56 home runs? <u>1997-8</u>

4. In which year did the American League leader hit only 40 home runs? <u>1994</u>

5. In which years were the fewest total home runs hit by the leaders in the two leagues?
   <u>AL: 1992   NL: 1995</u>

6. In which six years did the National League leader hit more home runs than the American League leader? <u>1992, 94, 98, 99, 2000, 01</u>

7. In which three years did the American League leader hit more home runs than the National League leader? <u>1995-96-97</u>

8. Which league's leaders hit more home runs over the ten-year period? <u>NL</u>

What Happened?

Directions: Look at the picture. Then, answer the prompts.

1. Make a list of **facts** (what you see in the picture).

   _____   _____

   _____   _____

   _____   _____

2. Make a list of your **thoughts** about the picture. (e.g., Why does the room look like this?)

   _____   _____

   _____   _____

   _____   _____

3. Write an **introduction** to your response.

   _____

   _____

   _____

4. Write a **conclusion** to your response, suggesting how the room came to look this way. Explain why you think that.

   _____

   _____

   _____

   _____

Go Around

> The **perimeter** is the distance around a geometric figure.

Directions: Compute the perimeter of each lawn in the problems below.

1. The Lawn Pros got a job edging a rectangular lawn that is 12 feet long and 7 feet wide. What is the perimeter of this lawn?

   _____

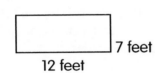

   7 feet

   12 feet

2. One neighbor had a lawn shaped like a pentagon. Each side was 9 feet long. What is the perimeter?

   _____

   9 feet

3. Mr. Cranky's lawn was shaped like a parallelogram. The shorter sides were 8 meters long each, and the longer sides were 18 meters long each. What is the perimeter?

   _____

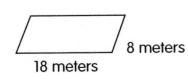

   8 meters

   18 meters

4. Dr. Cutter's lawn was a trapezoid with these lengths: 9 meters, 12 meters, 10 meters, and 17 meters. What is the perimeter of his lawn?

   _____

   12 meters

   9 meters   10 meters

   17 meters

5. The local dentist had a lawn shaped like an isosceles triangle, with two sides that were 8 meters long and a base of 5 meters. What is the distance around this lawn?

   _____

   8 meters   8 meters

   5 meters

6. The Grass Specialist edged a lawn with five sides. These were the lengths of each side: 9 meters, 7 meters, 6 meters, 12 meters, and 6 meters. What is the perimeter of this lawn?

   _____

   9 meters   7 meters

   6 meters   6 meters

   12 meters

Medical School

Directions: Read the following story, and then number the events in the order in which they actually happened.

This is Aaron's third year in medical school. He began medical school at the University School of Medicine after he graduated from Mount Vernon College. Now, he is both working in a lab and taking classes.

When Aaron was in the eighth grade, he visited a doctor on Career Day and learned that being a doctor was a great way to help people. Aaron decided that he wanted to be a doctor some day. He pursued his dream by going to college.

At Mount Vernon College, Aaron took a lot of chemistry and biology classes. Some of these classes were review, though, because Aaron had also taken chemistry and biology courses in high school. Also, while in high school, Aaron volunteered at the hospital, and these experiences helped him in college as well. Aaron worked very hard through college and earned good grades.

Although he is in his third year of medical school, Aaron has not yet decided what type of doctor he would like to be. Aaron enjoys research and may decide to use his medical degree to do research or teach. Aaron is glad that he decided to attend medical school.

1. _____ Aaron is working in a lab and taking classes.

2. _____ Aaron took a lot of chemistry and biology classes at Mount Vernon College.

3. _____ Aaron volunteered at the hospital.

4. _____ Aaron is in his third year of medical school.

5. _____ Aaron decided in the eighth grade that he wanted to be a doctor.

6. _____ Aaron began medical school at University School of Medicine.

7. _____ Aaron pursued his dream by going to college.

A Division Crossword

Directions: Solve each division problem. Write each quotient as a number word in the number puzzle. The first one (1 Across) has been done for you.

Across

1. 759 ÷ 69 = _____ | | _____
4. 432 ÷ 72 = _____
5. 348 ÷ 29 = _____
7. 120 ÷ 10 = _____
8. 156 ÷ 52 = _____
10. 185 ÷ 37 = _____
12. 528 ÷ 66 = _____
13. 273 ÷ 21 = _____
14. 504 ÷ 72 = _____

Down

1. 209 ÷ 19 = _____
2. 297 ÷ 33 = _____
3. 510 ÷ 85 = _____
4. 546 ÷ 78 = _____
6. 484 ÷ 44 = _____
7. 360 ÷ 30 = _____
8. 110 ÷ 55 = _____
9. 980 ÷ 70 = _____
10. 480 ÷ 32 = _____
11. 244 ÷ 61 = _____
13. 270 ÷ 27 = _____

Story Boxes

Directions: Choose a list of words from one of the boxes below. Make up a story using all the words in the list in any order you want. Edit your story for punctuation, grammar, spelling, and language use.

birthday party	ladybug	pizza	summer vacation
music	grassy field	Friday night	beach
invitations	tree	board games	sand castle
balloons	ant hill	friends	towel
cake	sun	soda	sunscreen
family	picnic	ice cream	bathing suit

_____

_____

_____

_____

_____

_____

_____

_____

_____

_____

_____

_____

_____

Food Challenge

Directions: Use the information in the recipe to help you solve the problems below. (*Hint:* Making a fraction of a recipe involves multiplication. Determining how many times a fraction fits into another number involves division.)

> ### Red Hot Chili Recipe (Serves 20)
>
> 3 lbs. ground beef   4 oz. chili pepper
> 5 lbs. beans   6 oz. hot sauce
> 4 lbs. tomatoes   20 oz. tomato sauce
> 2 lbs. macaroni   16 oz. water

1. Mary wanted to make only $\frac{1}{4}$ of the recipe. How much did she need of each ingredient?

   _____ lb. ground beef   _____ oz. chili pepper

   _____ lbs. beans   _____ oz. hot sauce

   _____ lb. tomatoes   _____ oz. tomato sauce

   _____ lb. macaroni   _____ oz. water

2. Lindsey wanted to make only $\frac{1}{3}$ of the recipe. How much did she need of each ingredient?

   _____ lb. ground beef   _____ oz. chili pepper

   _____ lbs. beans   _____ oz. hot sauce

   _____ lbs. tomatoes   _____ oz. tomato sauce

   _____ lb. macaroni   _____ oz. water

3. Annette wanted to make only $\frac{1}{2}$ of the recipe. How much did she need of each ingredient?

   _____ lbs. ground beef   _____ oz. chili pepper

   _____ lbs. beans   _____ oz. hot sauce

   _____ lbs. tomatoes   _____ oz. tomato sauce

   _____ lb. macaroni   _____ oz. water

4. Chili beans come in $\frac{1}{2}$ lb. bags. How many bags of chili beans would Zoe need to make the original recipe? _____

5. Tomatoes can be purchased in $\frac{3}{4}$ lb. sacks. How many sacks of tomatoes would Jenny need to make the original recipe? _____

Green Thumb

Directions: Read the story, and then circle the correct answers below.

Kathryn had been working for hours in her grandmother's garden. It was a favorite pastime of hers. She loved the feel of the moist, warm dirt and the sound of the birds in the air. It had been a wonderful summer so far. Kathryn was anxious to see the fruits of her labor in the garden. She had planted all different types of flowers, and she was checking each day for a bloom from the green stalks poking their heads through the ground.

Things had not been easy for Kathryn. She had been fighting all summer. First, it was the soil. She had raked all of the rocks out of it and tirelessly removed any clods of dirt. She had added fertilizer and other additives to make the soil healthy and strong. Then, the slugs came along. Slugs and grubs were eating any plants and seeds she sowed. Finally, she fought the weather. After weeks of drought, the rains finally came, but then they wouldn't stop. Water had washed away the first crop of seeds. In despair, Kathryn stood outside dripping wet, setting up a net to prevent her soil from eroding. It worked temporarily.

Kathryn's grandmother took delight in Kathryn's hard work and diligence.

"It's going to pay off, dear," she encouraged Kathryn each time she arrived to work in the garden. "Your thumb is getting greener every day."

Kathryn always responded with the same comment, "My thumb doesn't look very green." Kathryn knew that she needed to be patient.

1. What would be a good title for this story?

    a. "Lost and Found in the Garden"   c. "Work Before Play"

    b. "Hiring Scarecrows"   d. "Gardening Is Hard Work"

2. What can you conclude about Kathryn after reading the passage?

    a. She is loved and adored by her friends.

    b. She is good at math.

    c. She is learning self-defense.

    d. She is hardworking.

3. Which sentence helps you answer the previous question?

    a. "It's going to pay off, dear," she encouraged Kathryn each time she arrived to work in the garden.

    b. Things had not been easy for Kathryn. She had been fighting all summer.

    c. Water had washed away the first crop of seeds.

    d. "My thumb doesn't look very green."

Favorite Meals

Directions: Read each clue. Use the chart below. If the answer is "yes," make an **O** in the box. If the answer is "no," make an **X** in the box. Then, answer the statements below the chart.

Clues
- ☼ Tina likes to drink water when she has tacos for lunch.
- ☼ Jay never eats hot dogs, but he does like shakes.
- ☼ Marie always drinks soda when she eats pizza.

	Hamburgers	Pizza	Hot dogs	Tacos	Shakes	Soda	Water	Milk
Sean								
Jay								
Tina								
Marie								

1. Sean eats _____ and drinks _____.

2. Jay eats _____ and drinks _____.

3. Tina eats _____ and drinks _____.

4. Marie eats _____ and drinks _____.

Decode the Plates

Directions: Many license plates are personlized with a special message. Can you decode the following license plates? Write your answers on the lines.

1.
URNIZ

2.
IM182DAY

3.
IM4IT

4.
YRUHRE

5.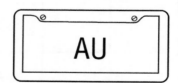
BLKNBLU

6.
BTTRFLI

7.
AU

8.
IM4ANTQS

9.
CR8Z4U

10.
CRUZN4U

11.
EZDUZIT

12.
URBZ

Solve Them

Week 3: Monday

Directions: Solve the problems. Show your work.

1. Mr. Garcia bought a truck that cost $28,500, including tax, title, license, and interest. He will have 60 equal payments until the truck is paid off. How much will he pay each month? Select the correct operation below, and find out Mr. Garcia's monthly truck payment.

A. Addition	B. Subtraction	C. Division	D. Multiplication
$28,500 + 60 $ _____	$28,500 − 60 $ _____	$60\overline{)\$28,500}$ $ _____	$28,500 x 60 $ _____

2.
$$\frac{4}{6} \times \frac{1}{5} = \underline{\qquad}$$

3.
$$\frac{2}{3} \times \frac{4}{5} = \underline{\qquad}$$

4.
$$\frac{3}{4} \times \frac{1}{2} = \underline{\qquad}$$

5. Each group of 4 students needs a bottle of glue and 6 sheets of construction paper for an art project. If there are 24 students in the class, how many sheets of paper will be needed altogether? How many bottles of glue will be needed?

_____ sheets of paper and _____ bottles of glue

6. For a Valentine's Day gift, Robin received a box of chocolates from her husband. There were 54 pieces of candy in the box. Robin ate 6 pieces of candy. Write the fraction on the line below that shows the number of candies still in the box.

_____

Madame Curie

Directions: Read the story, and then circle the correct answers below.

Madame Curie, also known as Marie Curie, was a great scientist who made many important discoveries. Her story is one of inspiration and determination. She was born Maria Sklodowska on November 7, 1867, in Warsaw, Poland. Poland was in turmoil, and her family struggled to make ends meet. Maria's parents were teachers, and they taught their children the importance of school. Maria went on to graduate with honors from high school at sixteen years old. She lost her mother and her oldest sister to disease, and Maria struggled with a nervous illness. She went to the countryside to live with cousins.

Maria returned to Warsaw where she and her sister attended a "floating university." The classes were held at night, and they had to avoid being caught by the police. They eventually left for Paris where she received a degree in physics and math. It took many years, as she had to put her sister through school, and then she put herself through school.

Marie eventually married Pierre Curie. Madame Curie, along with her husband, discovered two radioactive elements. This work laid the foundation for future discoveries in nuclear physics and chemistry. She and her husband received the Nobel Prize for Physics. Madame Curie would go on to receive another Nobel Prize for Chemistry eight years later. Madame Curie was **credited** with making great strides in science.

1. Based on the reading passage, what interests did Marie have?
    a. how to win the Nobel prize
    b. how to run an experiment
    c. math and chemistry
    d. physics, chemistry, and math

2. Marie worked so that she could
    a. be trained in how to run experiments.
    b. graduate from school.
    c. go to school.
    d. put her sister through school and then herself.

3. What does the word *credited* mean as used in the passage?
    a. added to
    b. known for
    c. increasing debt
    d. disregarded

4. What is the main idea of paragraph three?
    a. Curie's discoveries and contributions to science
    b. Curie's family background
    c. Curie's love of science
    d. Curie's choice of partner and husband

Patterns

Directions: Solve the problems.

1. Mary received $50.00 for her birthday. At the mall, she bought two books for $5.00 each, a new shirt for $15.00, and a DVD movie for $17.99. Which number sentence is **NOT** a way to determine how much money Mary has left?

   a. $50 – $10 – $32.99 =

   b. $50 – $10 – $15 – $17.99 =

   c. $50 – $5 – $5 – $15 – $17.99 =

   d. $50 – $30 – $17.99 =

2. What is the rule for the pattern of numbers below?

   a. Add 8, subtract 15

   b. Add 15, subtract 8

   c. Add 15, subtract 9

   d. Subtract 9, add 15

   > 21, 36, 28, 43, 35

3. Wanda is on the swim team at school. Her coach keeps a log of the number of laps and the time it takes her to swim 100 meters. Each Friday, her coach gives her a copy of the log so she knows how well she did. Which statement correctly describes the table?

   a. Wanda swims three laps every four minutes.

   b. Wanda swims one lap every two minutes.

   c. Wanda swims seven laps every twenty-eight minutes.

   d. Wanda swims eight laps every six minutes.

Summer Log for Wanda		
Days	**Laps**	**Minutes**
Monday	2	4
Tuesday	6	12
Wednesday	5	10
Thursday	5	10
Friday	10	20

4. Look at the pattern of numbers below. Write the two numbers that should go next in the pattern.

   23, 31, 40, 50, 58, _____ , _____

Diamante Poems

A **diamante poem** is in the shape of a diamond. A diamante poem is a descriptive poem.

Directions: Describe the events listed below.

Event	Descriptive Words
First day of school	_____
Learning to ride a bike	_____
Having a slumber party	_____
Getting a new pet	_____
Family gathering	_____
Sporting event	_____

Directions: Write a diamante poem using one event listed above.

_____
(event being described)

_____ _____
(two words describing touch)

_____ _____ _____
(three words describing the tastes)

_____ _____ _____ _____
(four words describing the sounds)

_____ _____ _____
(three words describing the sights)

_____ _____
(two words describing the smells)

_____
(adjective describing event)

34

Vehicles Sold

Directions: Make a horizontal bar graph showing the following information, and then find the sums and the differences.

Sports Cars	61,917		Small Trucks	38,214
Minivans	41,945		Big Trucks	43,127
Station Wagons	73,958		SUVs	29,060
Family Cars	62,000		Small Cars	54,498

	10,000	20,000	30,000	40,000	50,000	60,000	70,000	80,000
Big Trucks								
Family Cars								
Small Cars								
Small Trucks								
Sports Cars								
Station Wagons								
SUVs								
Minivans								

1. Small Trucks + Big Trucks = _____

2. Sports Cars + Small Cars = _____

3. Station Wagons + Family Cars = _____

4. SUVs + Minivans = _____

5. Small Trucks – SUVs = _____

6. Family Cars – Small Cars = _____

7. Sports Cars – Big Trucks = _____

8. Station Wagons – Minivans = _____

The Best Definition

Directions: For each sentence below, choose the definition that matches the way the boldfaced word is used in the sentence.

1. Senator Whistler took the **floor** to defend his position on the immigration bill.

    a. to knock down
    b. upper or uppermost surface
    c. right to address an assembly

2. Professor Watkins went to Australia to participate in the **dig**.

    a. an archaeological site
    b. to learn or discover
    c. to break up, turn over, or remove

3. My faithful friend Lindsey was a **rock** and stayed with me the entire time.

    a. move back and forth; zigzag
    b. stable, firm, dependable one
    c. naturally formed mineral

4. Attorney William Joseph's **opposite** in the case was Attorney Justine Modigliani.

    a. one that is contrary to another
    b. located directly behind or ahead of
    c. an antonym

5. Catherine Laws, my sixth-grade teacher, **holds** a degree in music.

    a. to restrain; curb
    b. to possess
    c. to regard or consider

6. When we went sailing on Saturday, the seas were very **heavy**.

    a. weighted down; burdened
    b. of great intensity
    c. violent, rough

7. The argument between the two wealthy adversaries quickly became **heated**.

    a. warm a building
    b. degree of warmth or hotness
    c. intense, angry

8. The nomination committee decided to **block** the investigation of their decisions.

    a. to impede the passage of
    b. to support or strengthen
    c. to indicate broadly; sketch

Family Vacations

Directions: Make a horizontal bar graph showing the following information, and then find the sums and the differences.

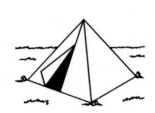

Beach	68,585	Camping	51,541
Road Trip	47,371	Big City	21,230
Mountains	32,371	Cruise	65,460
Stay Home	10,111	Another Country	16,221

Another Country															
Beach															
Big City															
Camping															
Cruise															
Mountains															
Road Trip															
Stay Home															

10,000 20,000 30,000 40,000 50,000 60,000 70,000 80,000

1. Beach + Stay Home = _____

2. Mountains + Camping = _____

3. Road Trip + Big City = _____

4. Cruise + Another Country = _____

5. Another Country – Stay Home = _____

6. Road Trip – Mountains = _____

7. Beach – Cruise = _____

8. Camping – Big City = _____

Pros and Cons

Directions: Choose one of the topics below. Then, write three statements for it and three arguments against it.

> ✿ Every child should walk to school.
>
> ✿ All boys should play football.
>
> ✿ Everyone should learn to ride a bicycle.
>
> ✿ Students should not watch television during the week.
>
> ✿ Winter school holidays should be longer and summer holidays shorter.

Pros

1. _____

   _____

2. _____

   _____

3. _____

   _____

Cons

1. _____

   _____

2. _____

   _____

3. _____

   _____

What's the Message?

Directions: Use the alphabet code to decode the message below.

A	=	26	N	=	13
B	=	25	O	=	12
C	=	24	P	=	11
D	=	23	Q	=	10
E	=	22	R	=	9
F	=	21	S	=	8
G	=	20	T	=	7
H	=	19	U	=	6
I	=	18	V	=	5
J	=	17	W	=	4
K	=	16	X	=	3
L	=	15	Y	=	2
M	=	14	Z	=	1

___ ___ ___ ___   ___
14 26 16 22   26

___ ___ ___ ___ ___ ___ ___ ___ ___
23 18 21 21 22 9   22 13 24 22

___ ___ ___ ___ ___!
7   12 23 26 2

Directions: Now, decode this message. (*Challenge*: Can you do it without using the code?)

___ ___ ___ ___ ___ ___   ___ ___ ___
15 18 8   7   22 13   26 13 23

___ ___ ___ ___ ___.
15 22 26 9   13

Silly Sayings

Directions: Each box below contains a common saying. Study each box, and write the saying on the line.

BAN/ANA

stand
👁

HORoB**OD**

M1Y L1I1F1E

Rosie

out

number Crossword

Directions: Solve each problem. Write each answer in the number puzzle.

Across

1. 942,977 − 861,165 = _____

4. 2,905,918 + 7,088,910 = _____

5. 336,073 + 400,368 = _____

6. 860,818 − 772,655 = _____

8. 448,231 + 114,474 = _____

10. 909,242 − 822,724 = _____

12. 730,598 − 693,107 = _____

14. 6,313,865 + 2,695,245 = _____

16. 1,650,039 − 1,224,916 = _____

18. 718,419 − 347,552 = _____

19. 5,947,045 + 3,795,684 = _____

Down

1. 6,419,280 − 5,601,491 = _____

2. 156,513 + 709,569 _____

3. 2,086,126 + 2,877,237 = _____

7. 972,657 − 816,578 = _____

9. 2,683,045 + 5,083,865 = _____

11. 2,456,038 + 6,304,895 = _____

13. 8,184,722 − 7,995,005 = _____

15. 135,683 + 791,334 = _____

17. 6,542,311 − 6,213,935 = _____

Cause and Effect

Writing

Directions: Match each cause with its likely effect.

1. _____ The car alarm went off.

2. _____ The lady drove very fast.

3. _____ He threw the watermelon.

4. _____ She gave the plant too much water.

5. _____ The electricity went out.

a. The policeman gave her a ticket.

b. The children ran away from the car.

c. The alarm clock didn't ring.

d. There was a puddle of water.

e. The watermelon split.

Directions: Write possible causes for the following effects.

6. _____ , so we left the movie theater early.

7. _____ , so I had to call my mom.

8. _____ , so our teacher gave us a pop quiz.

9. _____ , so I went to bed early.

10. _____ , so I finished my homework.

Directions: Write possible effects for the following causes.

11. I had a headache, so I _____ .

12. He forgot to study for his spelling test, so he _____ .

13. She won tickets to the circus, so she _____ .

14. My dog is too big, so I _____ .

15. I am allergic to peanuts, so I _____ .

Multiplication Mystery

Directions: Solve the multiplication problems, and match the answer to the corresponding letter to solve the mystery. **What did the children discover in the rabbit's cage?**

1. ☐
250
× 12

2. ☐
45
× 19

3. ☐
275
× 15

4. ☐
63
× 8

5. ☐
57
× 6

6. ☐
90
× 20

7. ☐
165
× 25

8. ☐
36
× 14

9. ☐
100
× 30

10. ☐
450
× 23

11. ☐
62
× 78

12. ☐
33
× 3

13. ☐
11
× 9

14. ☐
100
× 18

15. ☐
18
× 19

16. ☐
300
× 10

17. ☐
63
× 3

18. ☐
33
× 36

19. ☐
150
× 20

20. ☐
38
× 9

21. ☐
75
× 55

22. ☐
297
× 4

23. ☐
87
× 25

24. ☐
171
× 2

25. ☐
72
× 25

26. ☐
57
× 7

27. ☐
145
× 15

28. ☐
12
× 78
!

P = 399	**R** = 10,350	**O** = 855	**J** = 189	**I** = 1,800
M = 4,125	**S** = 3,000	**T** = 342	**U** = 1,188	**E** = 504
Y = 936	**L** = 2,175	**B** = 99	**A** = 4,836	

Coral Reef

Directions: Read the story, and then circle the correct answers.

A coral reef is a beautiful underwater community filled with many different types of species. You can find fish, coral, sea plants, and much more. These coral reefs have been around for millions and millions of years. Recently, some scientists have started to believe that coral reefs may be in danger. Scientists believe that pollution and human **neglect** have destroyed more than a quarter of the world's coral reefs.

Some of the living animals that make up coral reefs are struggling to survive. For example, coral looks and feels like rock. This causes people to treat coral like rocks. But coral is actually made up of tiny, clear animals. These animals are called coral polyps. Coral sticks together to form large colonies. When coral polyps die, they leave a hard shell of limestone behind. Coral gets its color from tiny sea plants called algae. There is a delicate balance between algae and coral. Coral reefs provide homes and shelter for many sea animals and plants.

Pollution and bad fishing practices have caused harm to coral and algae. Another problem is the warming of the water. Algae cannot live in warmer waters, and therefore, coral loses its source of food and color. This process has been named coral bleaching.

Scientists are working hard to find solutions to the problems in coral reefs. Their goal is to protect and preserve this natural resource.

1. What is coral made up of?

   a. sea anemone

   b. tiny, clear animals

   c. seaweed and moss

   d. rocks and crevices

2. When coral polyps die, they leave a hard shell of

   a. calcium.

   b. helium.

   c. carbon dioxide

   d. limestone.

3. What does the word *neglect* mean as used in the passage?

   a. respect

   b. carelessness

   c. love

   d. attention

4. What is the main idea of this reading passage?

   a. to inform the reader about the uniqueness of coral reefs and their need for protection

   b. to inform the reader about how coral bleaching occurs

   c. to explain the difference between the two different types of coral

   d. to explain the life of marine biologists

Read-a-Thon

Directions: Look at the chart. It represents the reading and pledges of fifteen students involved in the Read-a-Thon. After reading the chart, answer the questions.

Hudson Elementary School Read-a-Thon: Room 3			
Student Name	**Total Books Read**	**Pledge per Book**	**Money Collected**
Acevedo, Jennifer	31	10¢	$3.10
Adams, Joseph	5	10¢	$0.50
Barton, Michael	61	5¢	$3.05
Duran, Louis	17	15¢	$2.55
Edwards, Marylou	47	5¢	$2.35
Harrison, Trevor	11	25¢	$2.75
Lee, Rebecca	40	10¢	$4.00
Logan, Casie	22	5¢	$1.10
Marshall, Barbara	9	50¢	$4.50
Peterson, David	102	5¢	$5.10
Ross, Kathyrn	58	10¢	$5.80
Rublo, Anthony	83	5¢	$4.15
Shea, Sharon	39	10¢	$3.90
Tran, Alvin	14	10¢	$1.40
Yetter, Liz	75	5¢	$3.75
Total		——	

1. Which student read the most books? _____

2. What was the highest amount of money collected by one student? _____

   Which student? _____

3. Who had the highest pledge of money per book?_____

4. Was the person who read the most books the same person who collected the most money? _____

5. Was the person who had the highest pledge of money per book the same person who collected the most money?_____

6. What was the total number of books read by all the students? _____

7. How much money did the students earn for the library? _____

More Cause and Effect

Directions: List four possible effects for each of the following events.

1. There was a half-an-hour wait to ride a roller coaster.

   _____

   _____

   _____

   _____

2. The working conditions at a local construction site were unsafe.

   _____

   _____

   _____

   _____

3. A pan of broccoli was left cooking on the stove, unattended.

   _____

   _____

   _____

   _____

4. A toddler has Dad's car keys.

   _____

   _____

   _____

   _____

5. Rain was forecast for the day of the class picnic.

   _____

   _____

   _____

   _____

Games and Birds

Directions: The following frequency table records the responses of fifth graders when asked to name their favorite table game. Study the table, and answer the questions below.

Game	Tally	Frequency
Checkers	ⅢⅠ ⅢⅠ |||	13
Chess	ⅢⅠ ||	7
Twenty-One	||||	4
War	ⅢⅠ ||||	9
Hearts	||	2
Old Maid			1
Chinese Checkers	|||	3
Solitaire	||||	4
none	ⅢⅠ		6

1. Which was the most favorite table game? _____

2. Which was the least favorite table game? _____

3. How many 5th graders didn't like any table games? _____

4. How many more 5th graders preferred Chess to Old Maid? _____

5. How many students participated in the survey? _____

Directions: This chart lists the wingspan (from the tip of one wing to the tip of the other wing) of some birds. Study the chart, and answer the questions below.

turkey vulture	72 inches	golden eagle	92 inches
black vulture	60 inches	bald eagle	96 inches
red-tailed hawk	54 inches	red-shouldered hawk	48 inches
sparrow hawk	23 inches		

6. What is the wingspan of the sparrow hawk? _____

7. Which bird on the chart has the widest wingspan? _____

8. Which bird on the chart has the shortest wingspan? _____

9. How much longer is the wingspan of the bald eagle than the wingspan of the turkey vulture? _____

10. What is the difference between the wingspans of the red-tailed hawk and the black vulture? _____

What Happened Next?

When you write about something that happened to you or something that you do, it must be in the right time order. Another name for this is **chronology**. The things you write about in a paragraph should usually be in chronological (or time) order to make sense.

Directions: Put the events below in chronological order by ordering them from first (1) to last (5). The first one has been done for you.

A.
___2___ eat breakfast
___1___ get up
___5___ go to school
___4___ go out the door
___3___ brush teeth

B.
_____ bait a hook
_____ clean a fish
_____ eat a fish
_____ catch a fish
_____ cook a fish

C.
_____ mail the letter
_____ put the letter in an envelope
_____ write a letter
_____ wait for an answer
_____ seal the envelope

D.
_____ type a book report
_____ click on word processing
_____ turn on the printer
_____ turn on the computer
_____ print the book report

E.
_____ put anti-itch ointment on arm
_____ wash the bite area
_____ feel a bite, "Ouch!"
_____ hear a buzz
_____ scratch the bump

F.
_____ buy popcorn
_____ leave the theater
_____ stand in the ticket line
_____ buy a ticket
_____ watch a movie

G.
_____ find an old Halloween mask
_____ clean up your room
_____ sneak up on your brother
_____ put it on
_____ jump out at him

H.
_____ snap on the leash
_____ guide your dog back home
_____ get the leash
_____ whistle for your dog
_____ walk your dog

ABC Puzzlers

Directions: Determine the hidden meaning of each clue. Each initial below represents a key word. Find the missing words. The first one has been done for you.

1. 8 P in the SS _eight planets in the solar system_ _____

2. 26 L in the A _____

3. 52 W in a Y _____

4. TE invented the LB _____

5. A 4LC means GL _____

6. 52 C in a D _____

7. 4 Q in a D _____

8. 3 sides on a T, but 4 sides on a S _____

9. 7 C on planet E _____

10. An I has 6 L, but a S has 8 L _____

11. At 32 D, water F _____

12. GW was the first P _____

13. 360 D in a C _____

14. 64 S on a CB _____

15. 4 S on a V, but 6 S on a G _____

16. A U has 1 W, but a B has 2 W _____

Hidden Animals

Directions: Hidden in each sentence is the name of an animal. Each can be found either in the middle of a word or by combining the end of one word with the beginning of the next. Underline the animal name in each sentence. The first one has been done for you.

1. To and <u>fro g</u>oes the pendulum.

2. Oran came late to the party.

3. They do good work.

4. I can go at 6:30.

5. Steffi should be pleased with the results.

6. Magnus ate a whole bowl of popcorn.

7. Please allow me to help you.

8. We will leave for the picnic at noon.

9. She can't stand to be around cigarette smoke.

10. The teacher made Ernie stay after school.

11. Sheryl, I only have 50 cents in my pocket.

12. Sarah entered the church quietly.

13. Try some of these green grapes.

14. Is Mr. Roy Stern our new teacher?

15. They abhor senseless violence.

16. Cedric owns a sporting goods store.

Favorite Sports

Math

Directions: This pictograph represents a survey of sports preferences among grade school students in the 4th through 6th grades. Study the pictograph, and answer the questions below.

Students' Favorite Sports

Baseball	◯ ◯ ◖
Soccer	◯ ◯ ◯ ◯ ◯ ◯
Football	◯ ◯ ◯ ◯ ◖
Basketball	◯ ◯ ◯ ◯ ◯
Swimming	◯ ◖
Bicycling	◯

Key = ◯ = 10 students

1. How many students prefer to play basketball? _____

2. How many students prefer bicycling as their favorite sport? _____

3. How many students prefer to play baseball? _____

4. How many students prefer football as their favorite sport? _____

5. Which are the two most favorite sports? _____

6. Which are the two least favorite sports? _____

7. How many more students prefer soccer to swimming? _____

8. How many more students prefer football to baseball? _____

Electricity

Directions: Read the story, and then circle the correct answers.

We use electricity every day. We use it to light lamps, run the dryer, and toast our bread. We need it for our computers and TVs. There are times that we need more electricity than can be made. All electricity gets generated in a power plant. When we try to use more electricity than the plant can produce at one time, we have blackouts. The power goes off completely.

Wires carry electricity from power plants to your home. Some things, like copper, let electricity flow through them. These are called conductors. Electric wires are copper. Other things, like rubber, stop electricity. Power does not pass through them. These are called insulators. Copper wires have rubber covers to keep the electricity from leaving the wire.

Lightning is natural electricity. A single lightning bolt has **tremendous** power. It could light up a city for one year. Scientists want to find a way to tap into this natural energy source.

1. What is a machine that would still work during a power outage (blackout)?

    a. an air conditioner

    b. a battery-powered radio

    c. a refrigerator

    d. a television

2. Why would a large demand for electricity cause a blackout?

    a. People can't pay enough money to get the amount of electricity they need.

    b. A high demand for power creates an explosion at a power plant.

    c. When the power plant is overwhelmed by demand, it shuts down.

    d. When the power plant is overwhelmed by demand, it starts using lightning for power.

3. Of the following choices, which would make a good insulator?

    a. rubber boots

    b. a metal pan

    c. a lightning rod

    d. copper wires

4. What does the word *tremendous* mean as used in the passage?

    a. very little   c. enormous

    b. surprising   d. tiny

City Grid

Directions: Study the city grid shown below. Notice where landmarks, such as the bank and park, are located. Notice which numbers are positive and which are negative. Note how the four quadrants are labeled: I, II, III, and IV. Use the information to answer the word problems. Remember, always go across before going up or down, and use the point for finding the coordinate.

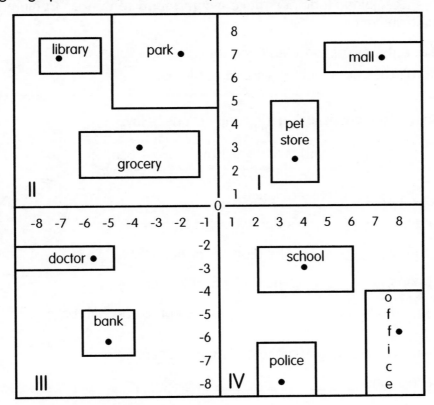

1. What feature is located at coordinate (7, 7)? _____

2. What building is located at coordinate (4, -3)? _____

3. What business is located at coordinate (-5, -6)? _____

4. Which quadrant has only negative coordinates? _____

5. Which quadrant has only positive coordinates? _____

6. What coordinate is shown in the police station? _____

7. What building is located at coordinate (-7, 7)? _____

8. What feature is located at coordinate (-2, 7)? _____

Join Them

Directions: Look at the information about compound sentences, and follow the directions for each section.

> Two simple sentences, joined together, make a **compound sentence**. **Conjunctions** help to combine simple sentences.
>
> **Example**: I bought apples, and Matt bought figs.
>
> Tom likes pears, but his sister likes plums.

Directions: Join the two sentences, using the conjunctions below.

> and　　　　　　but　　　　　　so

1. I am hungry, _____ I will eat lunch.

2. He wanted to go, _____ his dad wouldn't let him.

3. She called his name, _____ he didn't hear her.

4. Pia likes jelly beans, _____ she likes chocolate candy.

5. There's enough room in our car, _____ you can come with us.

Directions: Add your own sentence to make a compound sentence.

6. Jack played tennis, and _____ .

7. I eat lettuce, but _____ .

8. Saul wanted a pet bird, so _____ .

Directions: Join two sentences with a conjunction by drawing lines.

9. Tom wants to go in the pool,	and	you may go home.
10. Mia has black hair,		the pool is full.
11. The bell has rung,	so	I also like tea.
12. Greg knocked on the door,		he can't swim.
13. I like coffee,	but	Jacqui has blonde hair.
14. It rained heavily,		no one answered.

Just the Area

> ### Formulas
> **Area of a rectangle** = base × height
> **Area of a parallelogram** = base × height
> **Area of a triangle** = base × height ÷ 2

Directions: Compute the area of each lawn in the problems below.

1. Mr. Steven's yard is a parallelogram that is 9 feet high and 15 feet at the base. What is the area of his lawn?

   _____

   9 feet
   15 feet

4. Mr. Sharp's lawn is a triangle wih a height of 16 feet and a base of 17 feet. What is the area of his lawn?

   _____

   16 feet
   17 feet

2. Mrs. Frank's rectangular lawn measures 12 feet by 6 feet. What is the area of her lawn?

   _____

   6 feet
   12 feet

5. The Lawn Magician mowed their next-door neighbor's rectangular lawn which was 8 feet by 24 feet. What was the area of the lawn?

   _____

   8 feet
   24 feet

3. Mr. Ellis's lawn is shaped like an isosceles triangle. It has a height of 8 feet and a base of 6 feet. What is the area of his lawn?

   _____

   8 feet
   6 feet

6. Mrs. Potter's lawn is a parallelogram that is 8 feet high and 9 feet at the base. What is the area of her lawn?

   _____

   8 feet
   9 meters

Same Sound

> **Homonyms**, or **homophones**, are two or more words that have the same sound and often have similar spellings, but they have different meanings.

Directions: Select the correct homonyms from the parentheses to fill in the blanks in the sentences below.

1. Washington, DC, is the _____ of the United States. (capital/capitol)

2. To watch his sister Jane lose the race was more than John could _____. (bear/bare)

3. How many times have you _____ the doughnut shop without stopping? (passed/past)

4. Mother said, "Go to bed because _____ too late for you to be up on a school night." (its/it's)

5. "_____ going to clean up this mess?" my father asked about the spilled milk.
   (Who's/Whose)

6. The drum major _____ the band in the parade. (lead/led)

7. Do you think that the world will ever be completely at _____? (peace/piece)

8. The Wilson twins learned how to button _____ (their/there/they're) shirts
   when they were only _____ years old. (to/too/two)

9. I do not think it is _____ that my brother would not loan me bus
   _____. (fair/fare)

10. My editor does not think it is _____ that the judge will not allow me to
    _____ a newspaper story about the mysterious _____
    in which the barbarians participated. (right/rite/write)

Real World Geometry

Directions: Answer the following. Circle the correct answer or fill in the blanks.

1. Which street is **perpendicular** to Sam St.?

    a. Pete

    b. Jody

    c. Kyle

    d. Gordon

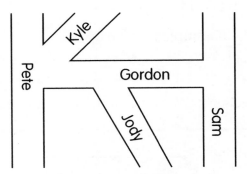

2. David worked on his racecar from 5:30 p.m. to 6:15 p.m. on Monday, from 6:10 p.m. to 7:00 p.m. on Tuesday, from 2:25 p.m. to 3:40 p.m. on Wednesday, and from 1:20 p.m. to 2:10 p.m. on Thursday. How many total minutes did David work on his car during the four-day period?

Day	Monday	Tuesday	Wednesday	Thursday	Total Minutes
Minutes					

3. Lee is buying a car cover for his son's jeep. The length of the jeep is 14 feet. He can buy the car cover in lengths of 96 inches for $21.50, 144 inches for $28.90, 180 inches for $32.60, and 240 inches for $38.75. Lee wants the car cover to fit snugly and to spend the least amount of money possible. Which car cover would be the most reasonable buy for Lee to make?

_____

4. What statement about the shape below is **true**?

    a. Side **MN** and side **QP** are parallel.

    b. There are no parallel sides on the shape.

    c. Side **QP** and side **NO** are parallel.

    d. Side **MQ** is perpendicular to side **QP**.

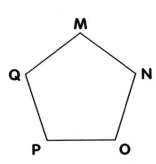

Fact or Opinion?

> Many sentences are statements. A statement begins with a capital letter and ends with a period.
>
> **Examples**:   I like apples.
>
> Mary sings pop songs.

Directions: Write a statement about each picture.

1. _____ _____ _____ _____	2. _____ _____ _____ _____
3. _____ _____ _____ _____	4. _____ _____ _____ _____

Directions: Decide if these sentences are *facts* (true) or *opinions* (what someone thinks is true). Then, write **fact** or **opinion** on the lines.

5. Sacramento is the capital of California.   _____

6. Water boils at 100 degrees Celsius.   _____

7. The koala is Australia's favorite native animal.   _____

8. Eating an apple a day will keep you healthy.   _____

Directions: Write one fact and one opinion about one of the topics above.

9. _____

10. _____

Droodles

Droodles are artistic interpretations of brainteasers. Pictures or illustrations are used to present information. Symbols may represent different things depending on the context. Word clues may be added.

Directions: What could these droodles be? Write your answers on the lines. The first one has been done for you.

Droodle #1

What could it be? _a slice of cheese pizza topped with sausage bits_

Droodle #2

What could it be? _____

Droodle #3

What could it be? _____

Droodle #4

What could it be? _____

Droodle #5

What could it be? _____

Droodle #6

What could it be? _____

If True, Then Do

Directions: To solve the puzzle and find the hidden word, read the sentences below. If the statement is true, then color the numbered puzzle spaces as directed.

11	7	8	10	2	4	1	13
4	14	5	6	12	15	12	14	4	16
12	1	3	13	8	11	8	16	5	15
9	6	5	2	3	9	13

- ☼ If cows give milk, color the #1 spaces.
- ☼ If whales swim, color the #2 spaces.
- ☼ If birds have scales, color the #3 spaces.
- ☼ If worms have feet, color the #4 spaces.
- ☼ If lions have stripes, color the #5 spaces.
- ☼ If camels have humps, color the #6 spaces.
- ☼ If pigs "oink," color the #7 spaces.
- ☼ If snakes are mammals, color the #8 spaces.
- ☼ If squirrels eat nuts, color the #9 spaces.
- ☼ If elephants have trunks, color the #10 spaces.
- ☼ If zebras have stripes, color the #11 spaces.
- ☼ If chickens "quack," color the #12 spaces.
- ☼ If spiders spin webs, color the #13 spaces.
- ☼ If cats have fur, color the #14 spaces.
- ☼ If ants are insects, color the #15 spaces.
- ☼ If eagles have feathers, color the #16 spaces.

What word did you find? _____

Meet the Merkles

Math

Directions: Ernie and Mandee Merkles have several expenses to juggle as they adjust to life in their new home. The following table shows the budget that they must follow. Calculate the yearly amount of their budget below. Then, answer the questions that follow.

The Merkles' Budget

Monthly Billing Item	Monthly Amount	Yearly Amount
Mortgage	$1,522.45	
Cable TV	$75.40	
Electricity	$120.34	
Gas	$60.52	
Telephone	$68.95	
Cars	$650.39	
Food	$200.85	
Clothing	$102.09	
	Total Yearly Expenditures	

1. Now that the Merkles know their yearly expenses, they need to plan for their savings. They would like to save $45.50 a month. How much will they have saved by the end of the year? _____

2. Mr. Merkles would like to cut one of his bills in half. He currently pays $75.40 for the cable bill. If he cancels everything except basic service, his bill will be reduced to half of what he currently pays. How much would he pay for basic service? _____

3. What would be his yearly bill for basic service? _____

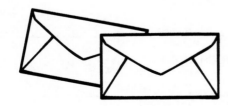

Let's Begin

> A **capital letter** is used for the first letter of a sentence, the first letter in proper nouns, and the pronoun I.

Directions: Color the boxes that contain words that should begin with capital letters.

asia	england	murray river	south	uranus
beetles	kansas city	october	stranger	vietnam
canada	london	pacific ocean	summer	wattle street
christmas	michelle	plate	swan lake	wednesday
easter	mount everest	shamrock hotel	tables	white house

Directions: Complete the sentences.

1. My full name is _____.

2. My birthday is in the month of _____.

3. The street I live on is _____.

4. The school I attend is _____.

5. My teacher's name is _____.

6. I live in the town or city of _____.

7. The country I would most like to visit is _____.

Directions: Rewrite the following sentences correctly.

8. last saturday julie went to chicago

   _____

9. at christmas we are going to italy, which is a country in europe

   _____

10. the wedding will take place at st patrick's church in greensboro

   _____

Rent an Apartment

Directions: Margo is about to rent her first apartment. She has estimated that she can spend up to $7,800 a year for the monthly rent. The following problems describe the things that she had to consider when trying to decide what apartment would be the best for her.

1. The manager of the Apex apartment complex showed Margo a two-bedroom apartment that costs $700 a month. What is the yearly amount for the rent? Based on her budget, can she afford to live there?

   _____

2. Margo saw a small apartment on the shore that she really liked. The rent was $680 a month. The landlord said that she could share the apartment with a friend. They would each pay an even amount of the rent. What would she have to pay for rent by the end of the year? Could Margo afford this apartment if she shared it?

   _____

3. Margo found an apartment near her job that costs $625.55 a month. It was a large space with two full baths and two bedrooms. She really liked it. What is the yearly amount of rent for this apartment? Can she afford this place?

   _____

4. Which two apartments described above can Margo afford? By the end of the first year, how much more would she have paid for the more expensive of the two apartments?

   _____

5. If the most she can pay is $7,800 a year, what is the most she can pay as her monthly rent? What division problem could be used to solve this problem?

   _____

6. What multiplication problem could be used to solve problem #5?

   _____

Micro- and Mini-

The prefixes *micro-* and *mini-* mean "tiny."

Example: *Microsurgery* means "delicate surgery done under a microscope."
Minuscule means "very tiny."

Directions: Write the correct word beneath its picture. The first one has been done for you.

~~microphone~~	microscope	microwave
mini terrier	minibus	minivan

1.	2.	3.
microphone		
4.	5.	6.

Directions: Circle the name of the item that's smaller. The first one has been done for you.
Hint: Two of these are tricky!

7. maximum	(minimum)	12. minute	hour
8. miniskirt	skirt	13. telescope	microscope
9. microfilm	film	14. raindrop	microbe
10. megaphone	microphone	15. mini terrier	St. Bernard
11. minivan	golf cart	16. toaster	microwave

How Many Degrees?

Math

Directions: Compute the number of degrees in each unmarked angle. Remember, the interior angles of a quadrilateral always add up to 360°.

1.

n = _____

2.

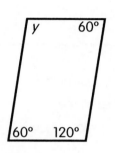

y = _____

3.

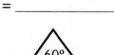

a = _____

4.

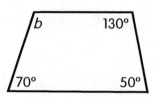

b = _____

5.

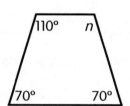

n = _____

6.

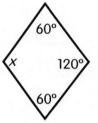

x = _____

7.

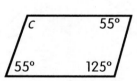

c = _____

8.

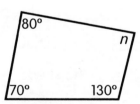

n = _____

9.

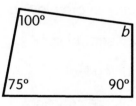

b = _____

10.

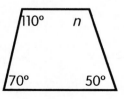

n = _____

11.

z = _____

12.

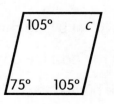

c = _____

Fill the Gaps

> **Prepositions** are little words whose job it is to tell about the position of someone or something.
>
> **Examples**: *across* the road, *before* the party, *up* in space, *under* my bed

about	at	down	of	to
above	before	during	off	towards
across	behind	except	on	under
after	below	for	over	until
against	beneath	from	past	up
along	beside	in	since	upon
among	beside	into	through	with
among	between	into	through	with
around	by	near	till	without

Directions: Choose a prepostion from above to fill in the blanks.

1. Wipe the glasses _____ a soft cloth.

2. Wait _____ the door, please.

3. The dog went _____ the gate.

4. Children are playing _____ the beach.

5. We learn to spell _____ school.

6. Did you look _____ the shed?

7. Ants are crawling _____ the hill.

8. A snake slithered _____ the log.

Directions: Rewrite the sentences, changing only the prepostion.

9. A cat sat by the chair.   _____

10. He ran past the door.   _____

11. She hurried towards the tree. _____

12. The truck went up the hill.   _____

Add the Lengths

Math

Directions: Compute the perimeter of these parallelograms. Remember, the perimeter is computed by adding the lengths of each side.

1.

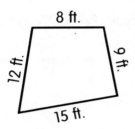

_____

2.

_____

3.

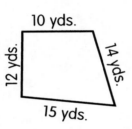

_____

4.

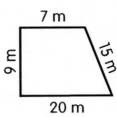

_____

5.

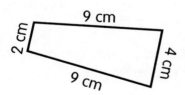

_____

6.

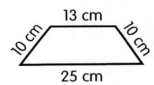

_____

7.

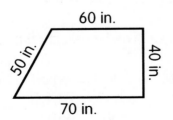

_____

8.

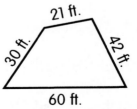

_____

Separate Them

> **Commas** are used to show short pauses in writing. They are used in various ways, including separating nouns, separating adjectives, and after introductory clauses and phrases.

Directions: Complete each sentence by using words from the Word Bank. Don't forget to use commas and capitalize the first word of each sentence.

Word Bank

ash	eucalyptus	pliers	scissors	tulips
corn	hammers	rice	skunks	wheat
daffodils	penguins	roses	sycamore	zebras

1. _____ are grains.

2. _____ are flowers.

3. _____ are black and white.

4. _____ are tools.

5. _____ are trees.

Directions: Each sentence contains a phrase that needs to be set off with commas. Insert the commas before and after the phrase. The first one has been done for you.

6. Adelaide, the capital of South Australia, is a beautiful city.

7. Anders Celsius a Swedish astronomer introduced the Celsius scale in 1742.

8. The South Pole a featureless spot in a freezing wilderness was first reached by Amundsen.

9. The toothbrush according to a 17th-century encyclopedia was first invented in China in 1498.

10. Ian one of this class's finest writers has won first prize in the poetry contest.

11. Interpol the first international crime-fighting organization was formed in 1923 near Paris.

Map Madness!

Do you see Peter? He is lost! Follow the directions to get him back on track. Mark his ending spot with an **X**.

Directions:

1. ⬅ Go west on Third Ave.

2. ⬅ Go left on Peach St.

3. ⬅ Go left on First Ave.

4. ⬅ Go left on Plum St.

5. ➡ Go right on Fifth Ave.

6. ➡ Go right on Pear St.

7. ⬅ Go left on Second Ave.

8. ⬅ Go right on Orange St.

9. **END** End at the corner of First Ave.

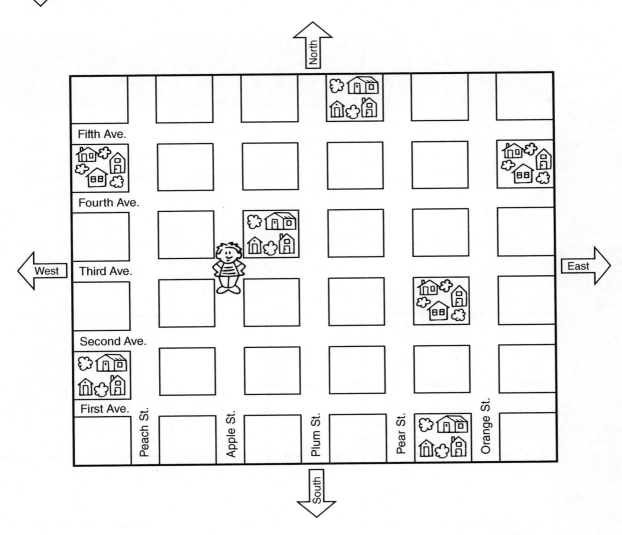

Race to the Finish

Directions: Mr. Jenson's P.E. class was running a mile-long race. Each student in his class had three weeks to prepare. Some of the students had practiced and some had not. Using the clues below, determine each child's place at the end of the race. Mark the correct boxes with an **O** and the incorrect boxes with an **X**.

1. Paul, who did not beat Emma, placed higher than Dan and Ellis.

2. Ben placed higher than Ellis and Liza.

3. Dan was not in second or last place.

4. Liza saw all of her classmates finish before she did.

5. Emma received the winning ribbon.

6. Ben was not in second or third place.

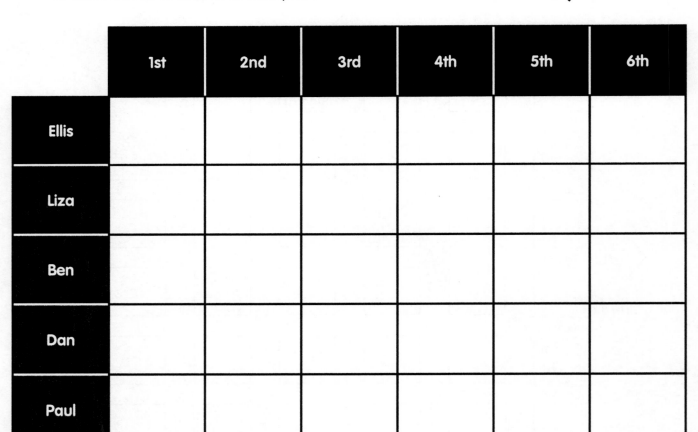

	1st	2nd	3rd	4th	5th	6th
Ellis						
Liza						
Ben						
Dan						
Paul						
Emma						

70

numbers and Dollars

Directions: Complete the following. Write each number in standard form, and then solve problem 5.

1. one thousand, four hundred, three _____	2. two hundred thirty-seven thousand, nine hundred, seventy _____	3. 2 thousands, 2 hundreds, 2 ones _____
4. 80 thousands, 9 hundreds, 1 ten, 8 ones _____	5. Kasey bought a present for her mother. She gave the cashier 4 tens and 7 ones. How much did it cost if she had the exact amount? _____

Directions: Write each number in expanded form, and then solve problem 10.

6. 1,256,753 _____ _____ _____	7. 38,281 _____ _____ _____	8. twenty-two thousand, six hundred _____ _____ _____
9. eight hundred forty thousand, three _____ _____ _____	10. Grant wants to buy a CD for $16.99. If he saves $4.00 a week, how many weeks will it take him to save enough money to buy the CD?  _____

Story Types

> **Fiction** is a story from someone's imagination. **Nonfiction** is a story that is true.

Directions: Read each sentence and decide if it would be found in a fiction or nonfiction book. Write your answer on the line. The first one has been done for you.

1. Columbus is the capital city of Ohio.   _nonfiction_

2. The Nile River is the longest river in Africa.   _____

3. It was a very stormy night when the aliens landed.   _____

4. Detroit is the home of the Ford Motor Company.   _____

5. A genie granted the girl three wishes.   _____

6. Space Rangers from planet Zoar came to the rescue.   _____

7. Your heart beats about 76 times a minute.   _____

8. Noisy squirrels threw a party in the forest glade.   _____

Directions: Read each paragraph below and decide if it is _instructional_ (describes a process) or _informative_ (reports the details of a significant event). Circle the correct answer.

This is how to make a grilled cheese sandwich. You need two slices of bread, cheese, butter, a knife, a stove, and a frying pan. First, butter one side of each piece of bread. Next, place one piece, buttered side down, in the frying pan. Then put one or two slices of cheese on that piece of bread. After that, place the other piece of bread on top, buttered side up. Finally, turn on the stove and grill each side for two or three minutes. Now you are ready to eat this tasty luncheon treat.

9.   **Instructional**   or   **Informative**

Florence Griffith-Joyner was once the fastest woman in the world. Her record times in the 100-meter dash and 200-meter dash still stand today. During the 1988 Summer Olympics, her speed, strength, and style helped her win three gold medals. Nicknamed "Flo-Jo," she was known for her beautiful, long hair and brightly colored fingernails. After she retired from competition, Florence Griffith-Joyner wrote children's books, designed uniforms for professional athletes, and served on the President's Council on Physical Fitness and Sports. "Flo-Jo" will be remembered as a remarkable athlete and as a productive private citizen.

10.   **Instructional**   or   **Informative**

Math Grab Bag

Directions: Estimate the degrees of each angle, and then solve problem 5.

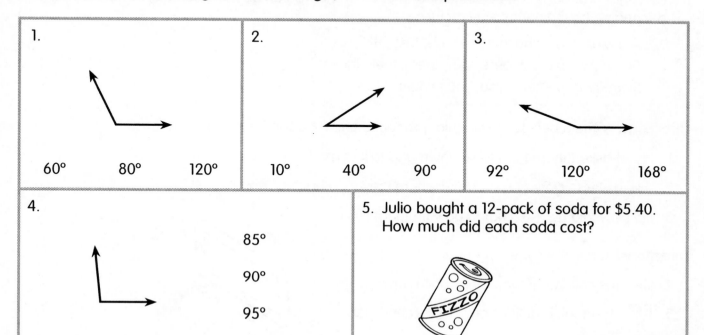

1.

60°   80°   120°

2.

10°   40°   90°

3.

92°   120°   168°

4.

85°

90°

95°

5. Julio bought a 12-pack of soda for $5.40. How much did each soda cost?

_____

Directions: Circle all of the prime numbers. Then, solve problem 10.

6.

23   46   21

7.

27   9   7

8.

11   20   15

9.

21   18   5

10. A car travels 65 mph. How far will it go in 8 hours?

_____

So Personal

> **Personal pronouns** can be singular or plural. Pronouns can be male, female, or neutral, depending on the nouns they replace.
>
> *Singular:* I, he, she, him, her, his, hers, it
> *Plural:* we, us, our, ours, they, them, their, theirs
> *Singular and Plural:* you, your, yours

Directions: Write **S** beside the singular pronouns and **P** beside the plural pronouns.

1. I ( ) asked them ( ) to sit down and talk to me ( ).

2. "Hello, Jess. Do you ( ) know where they ( ) have all gone?"

3. He ( ) told her ( ) not to go with them ( ).

Directions: Circle the correct pronoun.

4. Give the children (them, their) lunch now.

5. (Him, He) took a dollar from (his, him) pocket.

6. That bag of marbles is (my, mine).

7. The crow flapped (their, its) wings.

Directions: One pronoun has been underlined. Write the noun it replaces on the line.

8. Bess pointed to the boys and said, "<u>They</u> are making a raft." _____

9. "Will you give <u>me</u> a jelly bean, please?" asked Sean. _____

10. "Let <u>us</u> build a tree house," said Debbie to her friend. _____

11. John gave me the book and said, "Please put <u>it</u> on the shelf." _____

Directions: Write three sentences using these pairs of pronouns.

> you, him   they, them   we, it

12. _____

13. _____

14. _____

Many Variables

Directions: Find the value of each expression. Then, solve problem 5.

1. $x - 12 = 88$ $x = $ _____	2. $7 \times z = 49$ $z = $ _____	3. $144 \div y = 12$ $y = $ _____

4. $n + 120 = 241$ $n = $ _____	5. On the way to Mrs. Ward's classroom, the new student will pass four other rooms. Mrs. Proctor's room is next to Mrs. Baker's room. Mrs. Morgan's room is between Mrs. Proctor's and Mrs. Prince's room. Mrs. Prince's room is not next to Mrs. Ward's room. Which classroom is beside Mrs. Ward's room? _____

Directions: Solve for n. Then, solve problem 10.

6. $48 - 12 = 6 \times n$ $n = $ _____	7. $26 \times 3 = 122 - n$ $n = $ _____	8. $23 + 15 = 40 - n$ $n = $ _____

9. $72 \div 9 = 100 - n$ $n = $ _____	10. Sir Francis Drake explored California in 1579, and 28 years later, Jamestown was settled by Captain John Smith. What year was that?  _____

Air Tour

Directions: Read the following story. Use the Mini Dictionary to help you fill in the missing words.

Mini Dictionary

delta — a triangle of land built at the mouth of a river by the flowing water

hydroelectric — electricity generated by the movement of water

hydroplane — an airplane that is equipped to land on water

isthmus — a narrow piece of land connecting two large bodies of land

strait — a narrow passage of water connecting two large bodies of water

tributary — a river or stream flowing into a larger river or lake

---

A bus took us to the _____ between the two big islands, where a boat was waiting
                              1

for us. I'd never taken a boat ride to get into the air, but that's exactly what we did: it took us out

to a _____ just sitting there floating! After we climbed into the air, I saw two of the
          2

smaller islands connected by a land bridge, which the pilot told us is called an _____.
                                                                                      3

Before long, we were flying over the mainland. We started at the south, where I could see the

_____ of a big river. We followed the river north. At one point, I saw a big
        4

_____ dam, which the pilot said provided power for a whole city! As we continued
        5

north, I saw one _____ flowing into the river, then another, then a third. I was
                        6

sorry when the plane circled back to where we'd started for a landing. It was a great flight!

Directions: Match each idea to the correct word. Place the letter of the answer in the blank.

_____ 7. thin section of land   a. tributary

_____ 8. travels in the air, lands in the water   b. hydroelectric

_____ 9. makes power from water   c. hydroplane

_____ 10. thin section of water   d. strait

_____ 11. water on three sides   e. isthmus

_____ 12. flows into a river   f. delta

Shade and Show

Math

Directions: Shade each circle to show the fraction. Then, write > or < to make each equation correct. The first one has been done for you.

1.

$\dfrac{3}{10}$ ⟨<⟩ $\dfrac{11}{12}$

2.

$\dfrac{6}{12}$ ◯ $\dfrac{2}{3}$

3.

$\dfrac{8}{10}$ ◯ $\dfrac{2}{5}$

4.

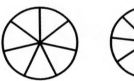

$\dfrac{2}{7}$ ◯ $\dfrac{4}{9}$

5.

$\dfrac{1}{8}$ ◯ $\dfrac{3}{7}$

6.

$\dfrac{3}{8}$ ◯ $\dfrac{7}{8}$

7.

$\dfrac{8}{9}$ ◯ $\dfrac{7}{9}$

8.

$\dfrac{6}{10}$ ◯ $\dfrac{4}{8}$

9.

$\dfrac{6}{9}$ ◯ $\dfrac{10}{12}$

10.

$\dfrac{1}{6}$ ◯ $\dfrac{1}{3}$

11.

$\dfrac{4}{5}$ ◯ $\dfrac{2}{10}$

12.

$\dfrac{3}{9}$ ◯ $\dfrac{3}{12}$

Which Kind?

Directions: Write each noun under the correct heading. Then, add two more nouns under each heading.

| book | cat | cousin | desk | girl | happiness |
| Houston | love | Spain | state | student | wisdom |

Person	Place	Thing	Idea

Directions: Write a sentence with each verb.

1. has taken _____

2. bought _____

3. has flown _____

4. went _____

5. have seen _____

6. walked _____

7. was going _____

8. is _____

Idiom Crossword

> An **idiom** is an expression with special meaning that cannot be understood by looking at the individual words.
>
>   **Example:** "With flying colors" means with ease and success.

Directions: Fill in the blanks with the words in the Word Bank to complete the idioms. Then, use the missing words to complete the crossword puzzle. The first one (2 Across) has been done for you.

Word Bank

bait	hour
~~bat~~	leg
bit	lost
double	switch
gun	time
hat	wire
horns	

Across

2. Right off the _____b a t_____ — immediately, spontaneously, and without delay

5. Make up for _____ time — to do much of something or to do something fast

6. Jump the _____ — to be hasty and do or say something before it is time

7. Take the bull by the _____ — to take action and stop hesitating

9. Shake a _____ — to hurry up and go faster

10. Down to the _____ — running out of time or at the last minute

11. Chomp at the _____ — to be impatient to start and enthusiastic to do something

12. Procrastination is the thief of _____ — If you wait, you may not have enough time left to do it once you finally get started.

Down

1. Fish or cut _____ — Do one thing or another, but stop delaying.

3. On the _____ — very quickly and at a fast pace

4. Eleventh _____ — at the last possible moment

7. At the drop of a _____ — right away, immediately

8. Asleep at the _____ — not attending to a job or not reacting quickly

Take the Plunge

Directions: Look at these groups of letters to solve the puzzles. They are in order, and no letters have been omitted, but most cannot be read left to right. Patterns may be horizontal or vertical. Pay close attention to the clues provided. The first one has been done for you.

1.
```
S  D  I
W  +  V
I  G  I
M  N  N
M  I  G
```
water sports

swimming + diving

2.
```
R  I  V  E  R
S  L  A  K  E
S  S  E  A  S
```
bodies of water

3.
```
T  E  S  T
U  K  T  H
C  I  R  G
K  P  A  I
```
diving body positions

4.
```
P  H  E  L
P  S  T  O
R  R  E  S
C  O  U  G
H  L  I  N
```
Olympic medalists

5.
```
S  H  I  S  M
Y  R  Z  W  I
N  O  E  I  N
C  N  D  M  G
```
water ballet

6.
```
S  P  R  I  N
G  B  O  A  R
D  +  P  L  A
T  F  O  R  M
```
types of diving boards

7.
```
B  A  T  H  I  N
G  T  I  U  S  G
O  G  G  L  E  S
```
swimmer's uniform

8.
```
S  A  A
P  N  M
E  D  I
E  S  N
D  T  A
```
needed to win

9.
```
N  V  R  W  M  L  N
E  E  S  I  A  O  E
```
important safety rule

Draggum and Pushum

Directions: Elliott Draggum of Draggum and Pushum's Pre-Owned Cars had a bit of bad luck. He accidentally threw out the receipts for the last six months of business. He needs your help to figure out the number of cars that were sold and the sales commissions for all of his employees.

Part I

In order to fill out the table, you must work backward. Read the information carefully in order to figure out the car sales for each month. You may have to read it more than once to complete the table.

March was a good month for car sales because they sold twice the amount they sold in July. Car sales in April and June were the same. April's sales were 20 cars less than in August. In May they sold 70 cars. In both August and July they sold 25 less than in May.

Six-Month Car Lot Sales Record

March _____

April _____

May _____

June _____

July _____

August _____

Part II

At Draggum and Pushum's Pre-Owned Cars, all of the sales people earn $250.00 a week as their base pay. In addition, they also receive a percentage of the sales price on all of the cars that they sell. Help Mr. Pushum figure out how much each person should be paid for the month of September. Complete the table.

Sales Person	Sales Total		Sales Percentage		Monthly Base Pay	Total Amount
Mr. Sanders	$45,000	x	10%	+	$1,000	
Ms. Elliott	$20,000	x	5%	+	$1,000	
Mrs. Shaw	$50,000	x	10%	+	$1,000	
Mr. Smitz	$30,000	x	5%	+	$1,000	

What Are They Doing?

Directions: Study the picture below. Record your observations, and then make inferences about what is happening in the picture. Provide evidence that supports your ideas.

My Observations

_____
_____
_____

Inference #1
_____
_____
Evidence
_____
_____
_____
Inference #2
_____
_____
Evidence
_____
_____

The Eatery

Math

Directions: Mark is the manager of The Eatery. He often has to change recipes to suit the number of people he estimates he will have to serve. Complete the tables in order to change the recipes to serve different numbers of people.

Party Fruit Salad

Serves 8 people	Serves 2̶4̶ people
6 cups watermelon	48 cups Wattermelon
2 cups raisins	6 cups raisins
3 apples	9 apples
$\frac{1}{2}$ cup cherries	1½ cup cherries
1 lb. strawberries	3 lbs. strawberries
1 mango	3 mahgos

Rule: ✗3

Turkey Loaf

Serves 8 people	Serves _____ people
2 lbs. ground turkey	
$\frac{1}{4}$ cup mashed potatoes	2 cups mashed potatoes
5 tbsp. breadcrumbs	
$\frac{1}{3}$ cup onions	
1 egg	
1 dash salt	
1 dash pepper	

Rule: _____

Chili

Serves 6 people	Serves _____ people
2 lbs. ground turkey	1 lb. ground turkey
8 oz. cooked black beans	
16 oz. cooked kidney beans	
$\frac{1}{3}$ tsp. fresh garlic	
$\frac{1}{2}$ tsp. salt	$\frac{1}{4}$ tsp. salt
$\frac{1}{5}$ lb. snap beans	
1 package chili powder	
1 cup salsa	

Rule: _____

Past Poetry

Directions: This famous poem by Robert Frost captures the feelings that go into the choices we make in our lives. We make choices like this every day. Think about some of the decisions you have made in your life so far, and write your response below.

The Road Not Taken

Two roads diverged in a yellow wood,
And sorry I could not travel both
And be one traveler, long I stood
And looked down one as far as I could
To where it bent in the undergrowth;

Then took the other, as just as fair,
And having perhaps the better claim,
Because it was grassy and wanted wear;
Though as for that the passing there
Had worn them really about the same,

And both that morning equally lay
In leaves no step had trodden black.
Oh, I kept the first for another day!
Yet knowing how way leads on to way,
I doubted if I should ever come back.

I shall be telling this with a sigh
Somewhere ages and ages hence:
Two roads diverged in a wood, and I —
I took the road less traveled by,
And that has made all the difference.

Decisions I have made today:

_____

_____

Decisions I have made in the past year:

_____

_____

Decisions I have made in my life:

_____

_____

How do you feel about these decisions?

_____

_____

Great Volume

Directions: Compute the volume of each cube.

> Remember, the **volume of a cube** is computed by multiplying the length of one side × itself twice. (V = s x s x s or V = s^3 or Volume = side cubed)

1. 4 cm

_____

2. 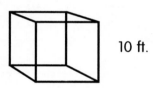 10 ft.

_____

3. 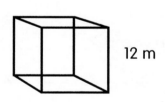 12 m

_____

4. 7 mm

_____

5. 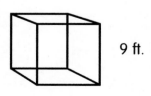 9 ft.

_____

6. 8 cm

_____

7. 20 mm

_____

8. 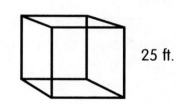 25 ft.

_____

9. 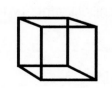 50 cm

_____

10. 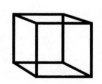 $\frac{1}{2}$ yd.

_____

TV Review

Directions: Choose a favorite TV show about a family. Then, complete the following TV program review.

Name of program _____

1. Summary of episode _____

   _____

   _____

2. Explain how the show depicts the mother. _____

   _____

3. Explain how the show depicts the father. _____

   _____

4. Name and describe a child who is a main character in this episode. _____

   _____

   a. What problem or dilemma does he or she face in this episode? _____

      _____

   b. How is it resolved? _____

      _____

5. Do you think the program portrays a realistic family? Explain. _____

   _____

   _____

6. How is your family like this TV family? _____

   _____

   How is it different? _____

   _____

Going the Distance

Math Facts

- ☼ The **circumference** (C) is the distance around a circle. (*Formulas*: $C = \pi \times d$, $\pi = 3.14$)
- ☼ The **radius** (r) is the distance from the center of a circle to any point on the circle.
- ☼ The **diameter** (d) is a line segment extending from one side of the circle to the other through the center of the circle.
- ☼ The **diameter** is twice the radius. (*Formula*: $d = 2 \times r$)

Directions: Label the circumference, the radius, and the diameter on these circles.

1.

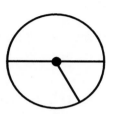

2.

3.

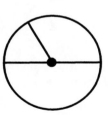

4.

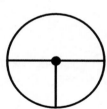

Directions: Use the information on the circles to find the values. Round each circumference to the nearest whole number.

5.

r = _____

d = _____

C = _____

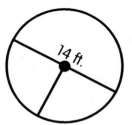

14 ft.

6.

r = _____

d = _____

C = _____

36 cm

7.

r = _____

d = _____

C = _____

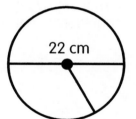

22 cm

8.

r = _____

d = _____

C = _____

42 in.

Find the Clues

Directions: The boldfaced words in the following sentences are unusual words. Use the context clues to figure out the meaning of each word. Write a sentence to explain what you think each boldfaced word means.

1. This is so **phenomenal**! I can't believe this mountain! I've never seen anything like it before!

   _____

   _____

2. Who made that **kerf** in the log? Whoever did it must have used a very big saw to make a cut that deep.

   _____

   _____

3. Elsa refused to wear flowers in her hair for her wedding because she insisted that they were **falderal**. Elsa felt that the flowers made her look silly and that they were unnecessary.

   _____

   _____

4. My coach is so **fastidious**. It seems like no matter how hard we work, she's not pleased.

   _____

   _____

5. I think I would have enjoyed the card game much more if my big sister had not been such a **kibitzer**. I got very tired of her hanging over my shoulder to give me tips.

   _____

   _____

The World's Best

Directions: Use the code to fill in the blanks and identify the person who is widely regarded as the world's best soccer player of all time.

A	C	D	E	I	M	N	O	R	S	T	B	Z	L	P	F	W
1	2	3	4	5	6	7	8	9	10	11	12	13	14	15	16	17

This soccer player was born in ___ ___ ___ ___ ___ ___ . At age fifteen, he played for the
                                              12 9 1 13 5 14

___ ___ ___ ___ ___ ___ , a professional soccer club. He was a talented
10 1 7 11 8 10

___ ___ ___ ___ ___ ___ ___ and led his team to three ___ ___ ___ ___ ___
16 8 9 17 1 9 3   17 8 9 14 3

championships. He ___ ___ ___ ___ ___ ___ ___ in 1973, but in 1975, he
                            9 4 11 5 9 4 3

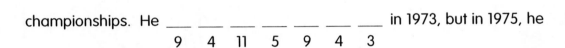

returned to play for the New York ___ ___ ___ ___ ___ ___ .
                                              2 8 10 6 8 10

The full name of the world's best soccer player is ___ ___ ___ ___ ___
                                                                4 3 10 8 7

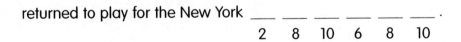

___ ___ ___ ___ ___ ___ ___   ___ ___   ___ ___ ___ ___ ___ ___ ___ ___ ___ ___ ,
1 9 1 7 11 4 10   3 8   7 1 10 2 5 6 4 7 11 8

but he is best known by his nickname, ___ ___ ___ ___ .
                                                  15 4 14 4

More Droodles

Droodles are artistic interpretations of brainteasers. Pictures or illustrations are used to present information. Symbols may represent different things depending on the context. Word clues may be added.

Directions: What could these droodles be? Write your answers on the lines.

Droodle #1

What could it be? _____

_____

Droodle #2

What could it be? _____

_____

Droodle #3

What could it be? _____

_____

Droodle #4

What could it be? _____

_____

Droodle #5

What could it be? _____

_____

Droodle #6

What could it be? _____

_____

All About Me

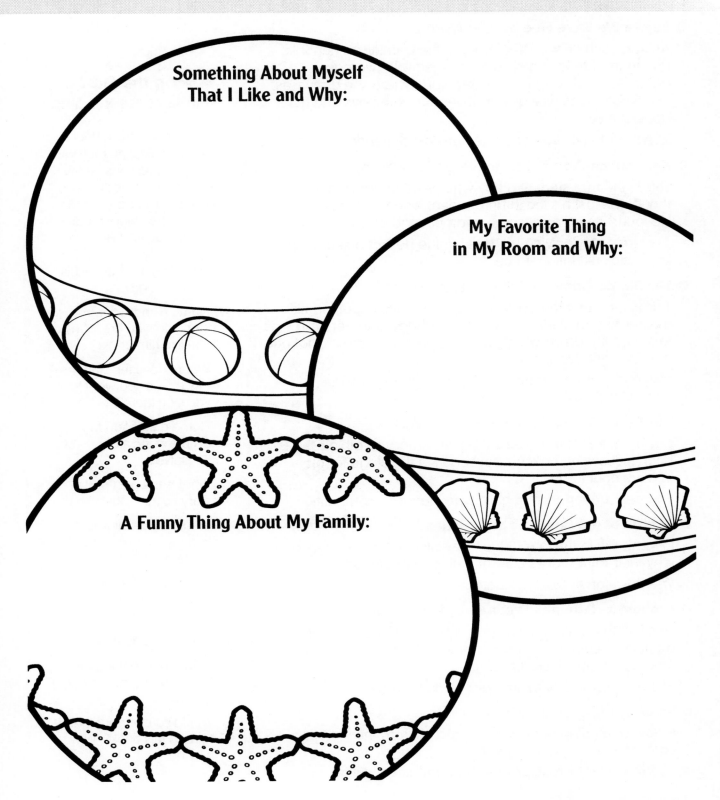

**Something About Myself
That I Like and Why:**

**My Favorite Thing
in My Room and Why:**

A Funny Thing About My Family:

Summer Reading List

○ **Before We Were Free** by Julia Alvarez

Anita must hide with her family in the Dominican Republic during the 1960s. She is a twelve-year-old average adolescent. She keeps a secret diary where she discusses her situation, as well as her obsession with boys and her appearance.

Themes: family ties, courage, the cost of freedom

○ **Knockin' on Wood: Starring Peg Leg Bates** by Lynne Barasch

This is the true story of a boy who loved to dance even though he lost his leg in an accident when he was twelve. He found a way to become a famous tap dancer.

Themes: never giving up, making the best of a seemingly impossible situation, fame

○ **The Shape Game** by Anthony Browne

This is the autobiography of a boy who accompanied his mother to a museum. It was her birthday, and her wish was to spend the day among paintings and sculptures. That one day changed his life.

Themes: the importance of art, changing view of life, understanding

○ **Jim Thorpe's Bright Path** by Joseph Bruchac

Jim Thorpe was the greatest Native American athlete. This book focuses on how his boyhood set the stage for his international fame.

Themes: importance of hard work, tenacity, competition

○ **Keeper of the Doves** by Betsy Byars

In Kentucky in the late 1880s, five sisters cannot understand why their father takes care of their scary neighbor.

Themes: family loyalty, kindness, empathy

○ **Leonardo: Beautiful Dreamer** by Robert Byrd

This is a fascinating biography of Leonardo da Vinci who was a painter, sculptor, scientist, mathematician, and architect. Award-winning illustrations.

Themes: inventor's mind, hard work, tenacity

○ **Vote!** by Eileen Christelow

Follow every step of the voting process from the start of a campaign to the voting booth.

Themes: Democratic process, importance of voting

Making the Most of Summertime Reading

When reading these books with your child, you may wish to ask the questions below. The sharing of questions and answers will enhance and improve your child's reading comprehension skills.

○ Why did you choose this book to read?

○ Name a character from the story that you like. Why do you like him or her?

○ Where does the story take place? Do you want to vacation there?

○ Name a problem that occurs in the story. How is it resolved?

○ What is the best part of the story so far? Describe it!

○ What do you think is going to happen next in the story? Make a prediction!

○ Who are the important characters in the story? Why are they important?

○ What is the book about?

○ What are two things you have learned by reading this book?

○ Would you tell your friend to read this book? Why or why not?

Summer Reading List

☼ **Chasing Redbird** by Sharon Creech

A powerful mystery story about Zinnia Taylor, a country girl who discovers a hidden trail and, along the way, discovers quite a bit about herself.

Themes: family secrets, finding yourself, mystery

☼ **Rodzina** by Karen Cushman

A twelve-year-old girl joins an orphan train and wonders what family will adopt her.

Themes: abandonment, values, dreams

☼ **Matilda** by Roald Dahl

Matilda Wormwood loves to read, but her TV-watching parents don't approve. Only Miss Honey, Matilda's teacher, recognizes her true genius. Matilda uses her head to help defeat the evildoers who are after Miss Honey.

Themes: problem solving, caring, positive attitude

☼ **Gandhi** by Demi

Gandhi's life and work is told in language easily grasped by elementary students. Beautifully illustrated.

Themes: humanity, humility, empathy

☼ **The Million Dollar Shot** by Dan Gutman

Eleven-year-old Eddie lives in a Louisiana trailer park with his widowed mother. A stroke of luck gives him a chance to win a million dollars by sinking a foul shot at the National Basketball Association finals.

Themes: poverty, life values, future dreams

☼ **The Year of Miss Agnes** by Kirkpatrick Hill

Miss Agnes arrives in a Native American village in 1948 Alaska and has a profound influence on her pupils.

Themes: learning, trust, friendship

☼ **Under the Quilt of Night** by Deborah Hopkinson

A young slave uses the Underground Railroad to make her escape to the North. Amazing illustrations help the reader to visualize this story.

Themes: courage, hope, friendship

☼ **Any Small Goodness: A Novel of the Barrio** by Tony Johnston

Short vignettes (chapters) make this a good choice for reading aloud. Arturo and his family leave Mexico for East Los Angeles.

Themes: family relationships, cultural differences, coping with difficulties

☼ **The View from Saturday** by E. L. Konigsburg

Mrs. Olinski's Academic Bowl team beats the older kids and makes history. Each team member has his or her own fascinating story, and together they are unstoppable.

Themes: teamwork, hard work, finding confidence

Summer Reading List
(cont.)

☼ **Sweet Potato Pie** by Kathleen D. Lindsey

An African American family in the early 1900s discovers a delicious way to save the family farm. Includes a sweet potato pie recipe.

Themes: close family relationships, working together to achieve a goal, ethnic cooking

☼ **A Corner of the Universe** by Ann M. Martin

Hattie's world is turned upside down with the arrival of a mentally challenged uncle. Set in the 1960s, it draws on the novelist's life.

Themes: difficult family responsibilities, making the best of a difficult situation

☼ **The Girl with 500 Middle Names** by Margaret Peterson Haddix

Janie realizes that everyone around her has more money than her family, who has recently moved to the suburbs so she could go to a better school.

Themes: life values, pride, family relationships

☼ **Dog-of-the-Sea-Waves** by James Rumford

In English and Hawaiian, this novel is about the first humans who set foot on the Hawaiian Islands. Manu and his four brothers must deal with this new land and then return home for their families.

Themes: man vs. nature, exploration

☼ **Holes** by Louis Sachar

Stanley Yelnats finds himself in a miserable juvenile detention center in the middle of the desert. While forced to dig holes, he also "digs up the truth."

Themes: finding yourself, courage, friendship

☼ **Maniac Magee** by Jerry Spinelli

This Newbery Award book chronicles a resourceful orphan who must make his own way in the world after running away from an impossible living situation.

Themes: race relationships, making the best of a difficult situation, hope

☼ **The Kite Fighters** by Linda Sue Park

It is 1473 in Korea, and an eleven-year-old boy and his older brother must deal with a rivalry when the older boy receives special treatment from his father as both compete in a New Year kite competition.

Themes: sibling rivalry, favoritism, family relationships

☼ **Tadpole** by Ruth White

Tad needs a home away from his abusive uncle. Even though his cousins are destitute, they welcome him into their home.

Themes: family love, abusive adults, gratitude

Fun Ways to Love Books

Here are some fun ways that your child can expand on his or her reading. Most of these ideas will involve both you and your child; however, the wording has been directed towards your child because we want him or her to be inspired to love books.

Write to the Author

Many authors love to hear from their readers, especially when they hear what people liked best about their books. You can write to an author and send your letter in care of the book's publisher. The publisher's address is listed directly after the title page. Or you may go to the author's Web site and follow the directions for how to send the author a letter. (To make sure your author is still living, do a search on the Internet, typing the author's name into a search engine.)

A Comic Book

Turn your favorite book into a comic book. Fold at least two sheets of paper in half, and staple them so they make a book. With a ruler and pencil, draw boxes across each page to look like blank comic strips. Then, draw the story of your book as if it were a comic. Draw pictures of your characters, and have words coming out of their mouths—just as in a real comic strip.

Always Take a Book

Maybe you've had to wait with your parents in line at the post office or in the vet's waiting room with nothing to do. If you get into the habit of bringing a book with you wherever you go, you'll always have something exciting to do! Train yourself to always take a good book. You might want to carry a small backpack or shoulder bag—something that allows you to carry a book easily from place to place. Don't forget a bookmark!

Novel Foods

What foods do the characters in your book eat? What do they drink? What are their favorite foods? Get a better sense of your characters' tastes by cooking their favorite foods. Some characters love sweet things, like cookies and ice cream. Other characters like hamburgers and pizza. Decide what foods your characters love. With your parents' help, locate appropriate recipes on the Internet or in books. Then, make up a grocery list. Buy groceries and gather necessary materials, such as mixing bowls, spoons, and pans. Cook your characters' favorite foods by yourself or with friends.

Write a Sequel

What happens to the characters in your book after you finish reading the final page? Why not create a sequel? A sequel is a book that is published after the first book has enjoyed success among readers. Sequels generally pick up where the first book left off. For example, the sequel to Madeleine L'Engle's novel *A Wrinkle in Time* is *A Wind in the Door.*

Bookmark Your Words

Make summertime reading lots of fun with these reading log glasses. Have your child fill in the glasses after his or her daily reading. Once your child has completed the glasses, he or she can cut them out and use them as bookmarks.

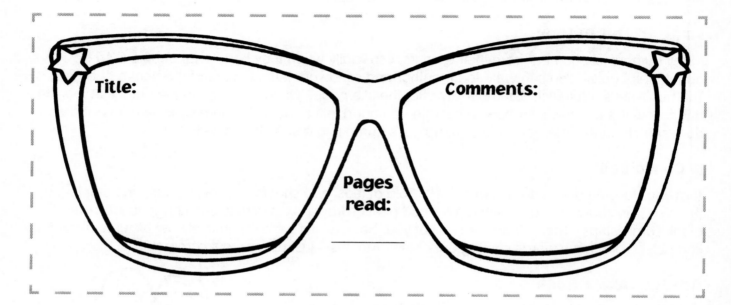

Title:

Comments:

Pages read:

Title:

Comments:

Pages read:

This page may be reproduced as many times as needed.

Read-Together Chart

Does your father read books to you before bed? Perhaps your mother reads to the family at breakfast? Your grandparents may enjoy reading books to you after school or on the weekends. You and your family members can create a Read-Together Chart and fill it in to keep track of all the books you've read together.

Here are two Read-Together Charts. The first one is a sample. The second one has been left blank, so you can add your own categories and books.

Sample Chart

Book We Read	Who Read It?	Summary	Our Review
The Secret Garden	My older sister read it to me.	It's about a spoiled girl who learns to love nature and people.	We like this book. The characters are funny, and the illustrations are beautiful!

Your Chart

This page may be reproduced as many times as needed.

Journal Topics

Choose one of these journal topics each day. Make sure you add enough detail so someone else reading this will clearly be able to know at least four of the following:

☼ **who**   ☼ **what**   ☼ **when**   ☼ **where**   ☼ **why**   ☼ **how**

1. One place I would really like to visit is . . .
2. The perfect pizza would be . . .
3. Right now, my favorite singer (or group) is . . .
4. My favorite athlete is . . .
5. My opinion of forbidding smoking in public places is . . .
6. The kind of school I would like to go to is . . .
7. One concert or show I really enjoyed going to was . . .
8. I would describe myself as a neat person (or messy person) since . . .
9. Exercise is important (or not important) because . . .
10. If I had to choose the college I would attend right now, it would be . . .
11. In order to become a great artist or musician, you must . . .
12. What I would tell a 3rd grader at my school about 4th grade is . . .
13. When I hear the phrase "practice makes perfect, " I think about . . .
14. A funny experience I had recently was . . .
15. A perfect summer day would be . . .
16. A fight or argument that I had recently was about . . .
17. A 5th grader should (or should not) get an allowance because . . .
18. A habit that I would like to break is _____ because . . .
19. A great amusement park ride is _____ because . . .
20. I would (or would not) like to be a doctor because . . .
21. In order to be a good friend, you must . . .
22. I wouldn't mind saving up money to buy _____ because . . .
23. If someone who didn't know my family asked me about them, I would say . . .
24. One television show worth watching is _____ because . . .
25. My favorite type of pet is . . .

Learning Experiences

Here are some fun, low-cost activities that you can do with your child. You'll soon discover that these activities can be stimulating, educational, and complementary to the other exercises in this book.

Flash Cards

Make up all types of flash cards. Depending on your child's interest and grade level, these cards might feature enrichment words, math problems, or states and capitals. You can create them yourself with markers or on a computer. Let your child help cut pictures out of magazines and glue them on. Then, find a spot outdoors, and go through the flash cards with your child.

Project Pantry

Find a spot in your house where you can store supplies. This might be a closet or a bin that stays in one spot. Get some clean paint cans or buckets. Fill them with all types of craft and art supplies. Besides the typical paints, markers, paper, scissors, and glue, include some more unusual things, such as tiles, artificial flowers, and wrapping paper. This way, whenever you and your child want to do a craft project, you have everything you need at that moment.

Collect Something

Let your child choose something to collect that is free or inexpensive, such as paper clips or buttons. If your child wants to collect something that might be impractical, like horses, find pictures in magazines or catalogs, and have your child cut them out and start a picture collection.

How Much Does It Cost?

If you go out for a meal, have your child help total the bill. Write down the cost of each person's meal. Then, have your child add them all together. You can vary this and make it much simpler by having your child just figure out the cost of an entrée and a drink or the cost of three desserts. You might want to round the figures first.

Nature Scavenger Hunt

Take a walk, go to a park, or hike in the mountains. But before you go, create a scavenger hunt list for your child. This can consist of all sorts of things found in nature. Make sure your child has a bag to carry everything he or she finds. (Be sure to check ahead of time about the rules or laws regarding removing anything.) You might include things like a leaf with pointed edges, a speckled rock, and a twig with two small limbs on it. Take a few minutes to look at all the things your child has collected, and check them off the list.

Take a Trip, and Keep a Journal

If you are going away during the summer, have your child keep a journal. Depending on his or her age, this can take a different look. A young child can collect postcards and paste them into a blank journal. He or she can also draw pictures of places he or she is visiting. An older child can keep a traditional journal and draw pictures. Your child can also do a photo-journal if a camera is available for him or her to use.

Web Sites

Math Web Sites

○ **AAA Math:** http://www.aaamath.com
This site contains hundreds of pages of basic math skills divided by grade or topic.

○ **AllMath.com:** http://www.allmath.com
This site has math flashcards, biographies of mathematicians, and a math glossary.

○ **BrainBashers:** http://www.brainbashers.com
This is a unique collection of brainteasers, games, and optical illusions.

○ **Coolmath.com:** http://www.coolmath.com
Explore this amusement park of mathematics! Have fun with the interactive activities.

○ **Mrs. Glosser's Math Goodies:** http://www.mathgoodies.com
This is a free educational Web site featuring interactive worksheets, puzzles, and more!

Reading and Writing Web Sites

○ **Aesop's Fables:** http://www.umass.edu/aesop
This site has almost forty of the fables. Both traditional and modern versions are presented.

○ **American Library Association:** http://ala.org
Visit this site to find out both the past and present John Newbery Medal and Randolph Caldecott Medal winners.

○ **Book Adventure:** http://www.bookadventure.com
This site features a free reading incentive program dedicated to encouraging children in grades K–8 to read.

○ **Chateau Meddybemps—Young Writers Workshop:** http://www.meddybemps.com/9.700.html
Use the provided story starters to help your child write a story.

○ **Fairy Godmother:** http://www.fairygodmother.com
This site will capture your child's imagination and spur it on to wonderful creativity.

○ **Grammar Gorillas:** http://www.funbrain.com/grammar
Play grammar games on this site that proves that grammar can be fun!

○ **Graphic Organizers:** http://www.eduplace.com/graphicorganizer
Use these graphic organizers to help your child write in an organized manner.

○ **Rhymezone:** http://www.rhymezone.com
Type in the word you want to rhyme. If there is a rhyming word to match your word, you'll find it here.

Web Sites *(cont.)*

Reading and Writing Web Sites *(cont.)*

☼ **Storybook:** http://www.kids-space.org/story/story.html
Storybook takes children's stories and publishes them on this Web site. Just like in a library, children can choose a shelf and read stories.

☼ **Wacky Web Tales:** http://www.eduplace.com/tales/index.html
This is a great place for budding writers to submit their stories and read other children's writing.

☼ **Write on Reader:** http://library.thinkquest.org/J001156
Children can visit Write on Reader to gain a love of reading and writing.

General Web Sites

☼ **Animal Photos:** http://nationalzoo.si.edu
This site offers wonderful pictures of animals, as well as virtual zoo visits.

☼ **Animal Planet:** http://animal.discovery.com
Best for older kids, children can watch videos or play games at this site for animal lovers.

☼ **Congress for Kids:** http://www.congressforkids.net
Children can go to this site to learn all about the branches of the United States government.

☼ **Dinosaur Guide:** http://dsc.discovery.com/dinosaurs
This is an interactive site on dinosaurs that goes beyond just learning about the creatures.

☼ **The Dinosauria:** http://www.ucmp.berkeley.edu/diapsids/dinosaur.html
This site focuses on dispelling dinosaur myths. Read about fossils, history, and more.

☼ **Earthquake Legends:** http://www.fema.gov/kids/eqlegnd.htm
On this site, children can read some of the tales behind earthquakes that people of various cultures once believed.

☼ **The Electronic Zoo:** http://netvet.wustl.edu/e-zoo.htm
This site has links to thousands of animal sites covering every creature under the sun!

☼ **Great Buildings Online:** http://www.greatbuildings.com
This gateway to architecture around the world and across history documents a thousand buildings and hundreds of leading architects.

☼ **Maggie's Earth Adventures:** http://www.missmaggie.org
Join Maggie and her dog, Dude, on a wonderful Earth adventure.

☼ **Mr. Dowling's Electronic Passport:** http://www.mrdowling.com/index.html
This is an incredible history and geography site.

☼ **Tropical Twisters:** http://kids.mtpe.hq.nasa.gov/archive/hurricane/index.html
Take an in-depth look at hurricanes, from how they're created to how dangerous they are.

Handwriting Chart

Aa Bb Cc Dd

Ee Ff Gg Hh

Ii Jj Kk Ll

Mm Nn Oo Pp

Qq Rr Ss Tt

Uu Vv Ww

Xx Yy Zz

Proofreading Marks

Editor's Mark	Meaning	Example
≡	capitalize	they fished in lake tahoe.
/	make it lowercase	Five $tudents missed the $us.
sp.	spelling mistake	The day was clowdy and cold.
⊙	add a period	Tomorrow is a holiday⊙
ℓ	delete (remove)	One person knew the the answer.
∧	add a word	Six were in the litter.
∧ (comma)	add a comma	He planted peas corn, and squash.
∿	reverse words or letters	An otter swam in the bed kelp.
∨	add an apostrophe	The child's bike was blue.
∨ (quotes)	add quotation marks	Why can't I go? she cried.
#	make a space	He ate two red apples.
⌣	close the space	Her favorite game is soft ball.
¶	begin a new paragraph	to know. Next on the list

Multiplication Chart

X	0	1	2	3	4	5	6	7	8	9	10	11	12
0	0	0	0	0	0	0	0	0	0	0	0	0	0
1	0	1	2	3	4	5	6	7	8	9	10	11	12
2	0	2	4	6	8	10	12	14	16	18	20	22	24
3	0	3	6	9	12	15	18	21	24	27	30	33	36
4	0	4	8	12	16	20	24	28	32	36	40	44	48
5	0	5	10	15	20	25	30	35	40	45	50	55	60
6	0	6	12	18	24	30	36	42	48	54	60	66	72
7	0	7	14	21	28	35	42	49	56	63	70	77	84
8	0	8	16	24	32	40	48	56	64	72	80	88	96
9	0	9	18	27	36	45	54	63	72	81	90	99	108
10	0	10	20	30	40	50	60	70	80	90	100	110	120
11	0	11	22	33	44	55	66	77	88	99	110	121	132
12	0	12	24	36	48	60	72	84	96	108	120	132	144

Measurement Tools

Measurement Conversion Chart

![cup]	cups (c.)	1	2	4	8	16
![milk carton]	pints (pt.)	$\frac{1}{2}$	1	2	4	8
![milk]	quarts (qt.)	$\frac{1}{4}$	$\frac{1}{2}$	1	2	4
![gallon]	gallons (gal.)	$\frac{1}{16}$	$\frac{1}{8}$	$\frac{1}{4}$	$\frac{1}{2}$	1

Inch Ruler Cutout

Directions: Cut out the two ruler parts, and tape them together.

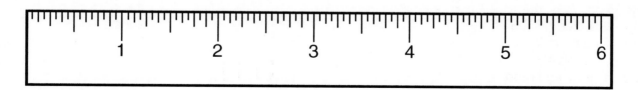

Centimeter Ruler Cutout

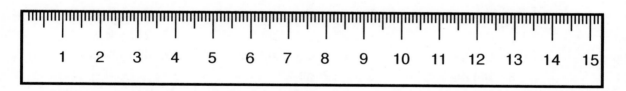

This page may be reproduced as many times as needed.

Answer Key

Page 11
1. $193.05
2. $12.09
3. $83.70
4. $11.99
5. $11.16
6. $250.00

Page 12
1. d   2. c   3. c

Page 13
1. Art Supplies: $2.00
   Snacks: $3.00
   Clothes: $4.00
   Savings: $1.00
2. $4.00
3. $2.00 x 52 = $104.00
4. 7 weeks

Page 14
Answers will vary; possible answers:
Main Idea: A successful road trip requires proper planning.
Supporting Detail: Decide how long the trip should be.
Supporting Detail: Plan your route on a map.

Page 15
1904   Ice-cream cone
1911   Oreo® cookies
1927   Television
1930   Pre-sliced bread
1969   Early Internet
1980   Rollerblade® skates
1981   Compact discs (CDs)
1993   Animal cloning—Dolly the sheep

Page 16
1. muscles
2. kayak
3. exhausted
4. navigate
5. collapse
6. d
7. a
8. b
9. c
10. e

Page 17
1. $4.24
2. $1.24
3. $8.51
4. $4.10
5. $7.23
6. $15.75
7. $67.50
8. $44.85
9. $4.94
10. $12.96

Page 18
Answers will vary.

Page 19
1. mild or dew
2. wind
3. hot
4. icy
5. season
6. sun
7. cold
8. heat
9. rain
10. thunder
11. cloud
12. tornado
13. clear
14. warm

Page 20
1. the dictionary
2. the newspaper
3. e, n, t (eight, nine, ten)
4. eleven (number of letters in the words "the alphabet")
5. Hawaii (People often say Florida, California, or Alaska.)
6. the letter "m"
7. She has all boys. No matter how you look at it, half of them are boys.
8. He was born in Room #1947 in the hospital.
9. Second place; Sandra still needs to pass the person in first place.
10. a tissue

Page 21
1. 2001
2. 1993
3. 1997, 1998
4. 1994
5. AL = 1992, NL = 1995
6. 1992, 1994, 1998–2001
7. 1995, 1996, 1997
8. National League

Page 22
Answers will vary.

Page 23
1. 38 feet
2. 45 feet
3. 52 meters
4. 48 meters
5. 21 meters
6. 40 meters

Page 24
1. 7   3. 2   5. 1   7. 3
2. 4   4. 6   6. 5

Answer Key *(cont.)*

Page 25

Page 26
Stories will vary.

Page 27
1. $\frac{3}{4}$ lb. ground beef
   $1\frac{1}{4}$ lbs. beans
   1 lb. tomatoes
   $\frac{1}{2}$ lb. macaroni
   1 oz. chili pepper
   $1\frac{1}{2}$ oz. hot sauce
   5 oz. tomato sauce
   4 oz. water

2. 1 lb. ground beef
   $1\frac{2}{3}$ lbs. beans
   $1\frac{1}{3}$ lbs. tomatoes
   $\frac{2}{3}$ lb. macaroni
   $1\frac{1}{3}$ oz. chili pepper
   2 oz. hot sauce
   $6\frac{2}{3}$ oz. tomato sauce
   $5\frac{1}{3}$ oz. water

3. $1\frac{1}{2}$ lbs. ground beef
   $2\frac{1}{2}$ lbs. beans
   2 lbs. tomatoes
   1 lb. macaroni
   2 oz. chili pepper
   3 oz. hot sauce
   10 oz. tomato sauce
   8 oz. water

4. 10 bags

5. 6 sacks

Page 28
1. d   2. d   3. b

Page 29
1. Sean eats hot dogs and drinks milk.
2. Jay eats hamburgers and drinks shakes.
3. Tina eats tacos and drinks water.
4. Marie eats pizza and drinks soda.

Page 30
1. You are nice
2. I'm 18 today
3. I'm for it
4. Why are you here
5. Black and blue
6. Butterfly
7. Hey you
8. I'm for antiques
9. Crazy for you
10. Cruisin' for you
11. Easy does it
12. You are busy

Page 31
1. C, $475
2. $\frac{4}{30}$ or $\frac{2}{15}$
3. $\frac{8}{15}$
4. $\frac{3}{8}$
5. 36, 6
6. $\frac{48}{54}$ or $\frac{8}{9}$

Page 32
1. d   2. d   3. b   4. a

Page 33
1. d   2. b   3. b   4. 67 and 77

Page 34
Answers will vary.

Page 35

	10,000	20,000	30,000	40,000	50,000	60,000	70,000	80,000
Big Trucks								
Family Cars								
Small Cars								
Small Trucks								
Sports Cars								
Station Wagons								
SUVs								
Minivans								

1. 81,341
2. 116,415
3. 135,958
4. 71,005
5. 9,154
6. 7,502
7. 18,790
8. 32,013

Page 36
1. c   3. b   5. b   7. c
2. a   4. a   6. c   8. a

Answer Key *(cont.)*

Page 37

	10,000	20,000	30,000	40,000	50,000	60,000	70,000	80,000
Another Country								
Beach								
Big City								
Camping								
Cruise								
Mountains								
Road Trip								
Stay Home								

1. 78,696
2. 83,912
3. 68,601
4. 81,681
5. 6,110
6. 15,000
7. 3,125
8. 30,311

Page 38
Answers will vary.

Page 39
Make a difference today!
Listen and learn.

Page 40
banana split I understand.
Robin Hood once in my life
Ring Around the Rosie white out

Page 41

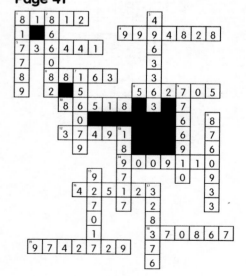

Page 42
1. b   2. a   3. e   4. d   5. c
6–15. Answers will vary.

Page 43
1. 3,000
2. 855
3. 4,125
4. 504
5. 342
6. 1,800
7. 4,125
8. 504
9. 3,000
10. 10,350
11. 4,836
12. 99
13. 99
14. 1,800
15. 342
16. 3,000
17. 189
18. 1,188
19. 3,000
20. 342
21. 4,125
22. 1,188
23. 2,175
24. 342
25. 1,800
26. 399
27. 2,175
28. 936

Answer: Sometimes rabbits just multiply!

Page 44
1. b   2. d   3. b   4. a

Page 45
1. David Peterson
2. $5.80, Kathryn Ross
3. Barbara Marshall
4. no
5. no
6. 614
7. $48.00

Page 46
Answers will vary.

Page 47
1. Checkers
2. Old Maid
3. 6
4. 6
5. 49
6. 23 inches
7. bald eagle
8. sparrow hawk
9. 24 inches
10. 6 inches

Page 48
B. 1, 3, 5, 2, 4
C. 4, 2, 1, 5, 3
D. 3, 2, 4, 1, 5
E. 5, 4, 2, 1, 3
F. 3, 5, 1, 2, 4
G. 2, 1, 4, 3, 5
H. 3, 5, 1, 2, 4

Answer Key (cont.)

Page 49

2. 26 letters in the alphabet
3. 52 weeks in a year
4. Thomas Edison invented the light bulb.
5. A four-leaf clover means good luck.
6. 52 cards in a deck
7. four quarters in a dollar
8. three sides on a triangle, but four sides on a square
9. seven continents on planet Earth
10. An insect has six legs, but a spider has eight legs.
11. At 32 degrees, water freezes.
12. George Washington was the first president.
13. 360 degrees in a circle
14. 64 squares on a chessboard (or checkerboard)
15. four strings on a violin, but six strings on a guitar
16. A unicycle has one wheel, but a bicycle has two wheels.

Page 50

2. camel
3. dog
4. goat
5. fish
6. owl
7. seal
8. cat
9. bear
10. deer
11. lion
12. hen
13. ape
14. oyster or newt
15. horse
16. cow

Page 51

1. 50
2. 10
3. 25
4. 45
5. soccer, basketball
6. swimming, bicycling
7. 45
8. 20

Page 52

1. b
2. c
3. a
4. c

Page 53

1. mall
2. school
3. bank
4. III
5. I
6. (3, -8)
7. library
8. park

Page 54

1. so
2. but
3. but
4. and
5. so
6–8. Answers will vary.

9. Tom wants to go in the pool, — the pool is full.
10. Mia has black hair, — Jacqui has blonde hair.
11. The bell has rung, — so — he can't swim.
12. Greg knocked on the door, — no one answered.
13. I like coffee, — and — I also like tea.
14. It rained heavily, — but — you may go home.

Page 55

1. 135 sq. feet
2. 72 sq. feet
3. 24 sq. feet
4. 136 sq. feet
5. 192 sq. feet
6. 72 sq. feet

Page 56

1. capital
2. bear
3. passed
4. it's
5. Who's
6. led
7. peace
8. their, two
9. fair, fare
10. right, write, rite

Page 57

1. d
2. 220 minutes
3. 180-inch length
4. b

Page 58

1–4. Answers will vary.
5. fact
6. fact
7. opinion
8. opinion
9–10. Answers will vary.

Page 59

Answers will vary.

Page 60

Zoo

Page 61

Mortgage	$18,269.40
Cable TV	$904.80
Electricity	$1,444.08
Gas	$726.24
Telephone	$827.40
Cars	$7,804.68
Food	$2,410.20
Clothing	$1,225.08
Total	$33,611.88

1. $45.50 x 12 = $546.00
2. $37.70
3. $452.40

Answer Key (cont.)

Page 62

Colored boxes: Asia, Canada, Christmas, Easter, England, Kansas City, London, Michelle, Mount Everest, Murray River, October, Pacific Ocean, Shamrock Hotel, Swan Lake, Uranus, Vietnam, Wattle Street, Wednesday, White House

1–7. Answers will vary.

8. Last Saturday Julie went to Chicago.

9. At Christmas we are going to Italy, which is a country in Europe.

10. The wedding will take place at St. Patrick's Church in Greensboro.

Page 63

1. $8,400; no
2. $4,080; yes
3. $7,506.60; yes
4. #2 and #3; $3,426.60
5. $650; $7,800 ÷ 12 = $650
6. $7,800 x $\frac{1}{12}$ = $650

Page 64

2. minibus
3. mini terrier
4. minivan
5. microwave
6. microscope
8. miniskirt
9. microfilm
10. microphone
11. golf cart
12. minute
13. microscope
14. microbe
15. mini terrier
16. toaster

Page 65

1. 90°
2. 120°
3. 90°
4. 110°
5. 110°
6. 120°
7. 125°
8. 80°
9. 95°
10. 130°
11. 100°
12. 75°

Page 66

Answers will vary; possible answers:

1. with
2. near
3. through
4. on
5. at
6. in
7. around
8. over
9. A cat sat **upon** the chair.
10. He ran **towards** the door.
11. She hurried **up** the tree.
12. The truck went **down** the hill.

Page 67

1. 44 ft.
2. 51 m
3. 51 yds.
4. 58 cm
5. 24 cm
6. 210 m
7. 220 in.
8. 153 ft.

Page 68

1. Corn, rice, and wheat
2. Daffodils, roses, and tulips
3. Penguins, skunks, and zebras
4. Hammers, pliers, and scissors
5. Ash, eucalyptus, and sycamore
7. a Swedish astronomer
8. a featureless spot in a freezing wilderness
9. according to a 17th-century encyclopedia
10. one of this class's finest writers
11. the first international crime-fighting organization

Page 69

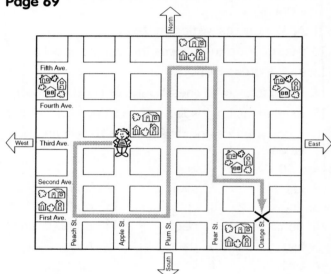

Page 70

Ellis—5th place
Liza—6th place
Ben—4th place
Dan—3rd place
Paul—2nd place
Emma—1st place

Page 71

1. 1,403
2. 237,970
3. 2,202
4. 80,918
5. $47.00
6. 1,000,000+ 200,000 + 50,000 + 6,000 + 700 + 50 + 3
7. 30,000 + 8,000 + 200 + 80 + 1
8. 20,000 + 2,000 + 600
9. 800,000 + 40,000 + 3
10. 5 weeks

Answer Key *(cont.)*

Page 72

2. nonfiction
3. fiction
4. nonfiction
5. fiction
6. fiction
7. nonfiction
8. fiction
9. Instructional
10. Informative

Page 73

1. 120°
2. 40°
3. 168°
4. 95°
5. 45¢
6. 23
7. 7
8. 11
9. 5
10. 520 miles

Page 74

1. I = **S**, them = **P**, me = **S**
2. you = **S**, they = **P**
3. He = **S**, her = **S**, them = **P**
4. their
5. He, his
6. mine
7. its
8. the boys
9. Sean
10. Debbie and her friend
11. the book
12–14. Sentences will vary.

Page 75

1. 100
2. 7
3. 12
4. 121
5. Mrs. Baker's
6. 6
7. 44
8. 2
9. 92
10. 1607

Page 76

1. strait
2. hydroplane
3. isthmus
4. delta
5. hydroelectric
6. tributary
7. e
8. c
9. b
10. d
11. f
12. a

Page 77

2. <
3. >
4. <
5. <
6. <
7. >
8. >
9. <
10. <
11. >
12. >

Page 78

Additional nouns will vary.
Person: cousin, girl, student
Place: Houston, Spain, state
Thing: book, cat, desk
Idea: happiness, love, wisdom
1–8. Answers will vary.

Page 79

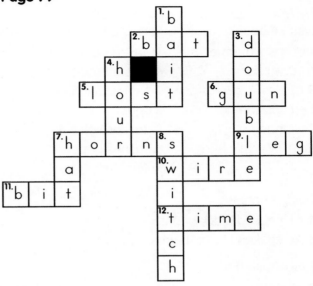

Page 80

2. rivers, lakes, seas
3. tuck, pike, straight
4. Phelps, Torres, Coughlin
5. synchronized swimming
6. springboard + platform
7. bathing suit, goggles
8. speed and stamina
9. Never swim alone.

Page 81

Part I

March—90
April—25
May—70
June—25
July—45
August—45

Part II

Mr. Sanders—$5,500
Ms. Elliott—$2,000
Mrs. Shaw—$6,000
Mr. Smitz—$2,500

Page 82

Answers will vary.

Answer Key *(cont.)*

Page 83

Party Fruit Salad
Serves 24 people

    18 cups watermelon

    6 cups raisins

    9 apples

    $1\frac{1}{2}$ cups cherries

    3 mangoes

    Rule: Multiply by 3.

Turkey Loaf
Serves 64 people

    16 lbs. ground turkey

    40 tbsp. breadcrumbs

    $2\frac{2}{3}$ cups onions

    8 eggs

    8 dashes salt

    8 dashes pepper

    Rule: Multiply by 8.

Chili
Serves 3 people

    4 oz. cooked black beans

    8 oz. cooked kidney beans

    $\frac{1}{6}$ tsp. fresh garlic

    $\frac{1}{10}$ lb. snap beans

    $\frac{1}{2}$ package chili powder

    $\frac{1}{2}$ cup salsa

    Rule: Divide by 2 or multiply by $\frac{1}{2}$.

Page 84
Answers will vary.

Page 85

1. 64 cm³
2. 1,000 ft.³
3. 1,728 m³
4. 343 mm³
5. 729 ft.³
6. 512 cm³
7. 8,000 mm³
8. 15,625 ft.³
9. 125,000 cm³
10. $\frac{1}{8}$ yd.³

Page 86
Answers will vary.

Page 87

1.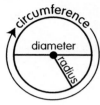
2.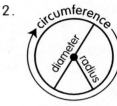
3.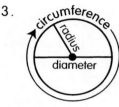
4.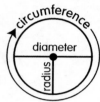

5. r = 7 ft.
   d = 14 ft.
   C = 44 ft.

6. r = 18 cm
   d = 36 cm
   C = 113 cm

7. r = 11 cm
   d = 22 cm
   C = 69 cm

8. r = 21 in.
   d = 42 in.
   C = 132 in.

Page 88
Answers will vary; possible answers:

1. *Phenomenal* means unbelievable and uncommon.
2. A *kerf* is a cut or incision.
3. *Falderal* is wasted effort and nonsense.
4. *Fastidious* means hard to please.
5. A *kibitzer* is someone who watches a card game and gives unsolicited advice.

Page 89
This soccer player was born in **Brazil**. At age fifteen, he played for the **Santos**, a professional soccer club. He was a talented **forward** and led his team to three **world** championships. He **retired** in 1973, but in 1975, he returned to play for the New York **Cosmos**.

The full name of the world's best soccer player is **Edson Arantes do Nascimento**, but he is best known by his nickname, **Pele**.

Page 90
Answers will vary.